Baghdad, Adieu

SALAH AL HAMDANI

Baghdad, Adieu

SELECTED POEMS OF MEMORY AND EXILE

TRANSLATED BY SONIA ALLAND

LONDON NEW YORK CALCUTTA

Seagull Books, 2018

First published in English translation by Seagull Books, 2018

Original poems from *Au dessus de la table, Un ciel* (Above the Table, a Sky); *Memoire de Braise* (Memory of Embers); *J'ai vu* (I've Seen); *L'Arrogance des jours* (Arrogance of the Days); *Ce qu'il reste de lumière* (What Remains of Light); and *Au large de douleur* (Beyond Pain) © Salah Al Hamdani

The poet and the translator are grateful to the following publishers for permission to translate poems from the following volumes:

EDITIONS BRUNO DOUCEY, for poems from *Le Balayeur du désert* (The Sweeper of the Desert); *Bagdad-Jérusalem, à la lisière de l'incendie* (Baghdad-Jerusalem, at the Fire's Edge); and *Rebâtir les jours* (Rebuild the Days).

LE TEMPS DES CERISES for poems from: *Adieu mon tortionnaire* (Adieu, my Torturer); and *Bagdad à ciel ouvert* (The Open Sky of Baghdad).

PIPPA EDITIONS for the poem from: *Je te rêve* (for You, I Dream).

AL MANAR for poems from: *Saisons d'Argile* (Seasons of Clay).

Translations © Sonia Alland, 2018

ISBN   978 0 8574 2 544 7

British Library Cataloguing-in-Publication Data
A catalogue record for this book is available from the British Library.

Typeset by Seagull Books, Calcutta, India
Printed and bound by Maple Press, York, Pennsylvania, USA

CONTENTS

Acknowledgements   *xi*

Translator's Introduction   *xii*

A Note on the Poems   *xxiii*

FROM *Above the Table, a Sky*   **1**

    Exit   3

    Summit of Passion   5

FROM *Memory of Embers*   **7**

  BUNDLE OF DAYS OVERWHELMED BY THE WAR   **9**

    The First Day   9

    The Fourth Day   9

    The Sixteenth Day   10

    The Twenty-Ninth Day   10

  BUNDLES OF WINGS FOR BAGHDAD   **12**

    Homage   12

    Story   12

  WALL OF EXILE   **13**

    FROM *I've Seen*   13

    Epilogue   18

    Letter   18

    After 6840 Days of Exile   20

FROM *The Arrogance of the Days*   **21**

  MEN   **23**

    The Second Man   23

    The Third Man   23

The Fourth Man   24
The Eleventh Man   24
The Seventeenth Man   26

THE HEIGHT OF THE DAYS   **27**
Baghdad   27
The Tenth Day   28
The Eleventh Day   29

NOTES ON THE WAR   **30**
First Look   30
Second Look   30
Fourth Look   30
Seventh Look   31
Twelfth Look   31

MY BLACK FLOWER   **34**
The Beacon of Makeshift Houses   34
The City of Sand   35
A Homeland   37
The Necrologist   38

FROM *What Remains of Light*   **41**
Who Makes the Wind Blow?   43
A Touch of Light   44
Words Have Bodies   45
Near Withered Time   47
A Monday Afternoon   48
Grave-Digger   49
Everything Passes   51
Act   53
Assembling   54
Give Back My Waiting   56
The Memory of Clay   58
Neighing Towards Baghdad   59
Still   61
Destiny   62

FROM *Beyond Pain* **63**

    5 January 65

    7 January 66

    2 March 67

    8 March 68

    12 March 69

    7 April 70

    28 June 71

    30 June 72

    3 July 73

    20 July 74

    25 July 75

    26 August, Jeu Les Bois 76

    12 November 77

    1 December 78

    2 December 79

    3 December 80

    4 January 2000 81

FROM *The Open Sky of Baghdad* **83**

POEMS BEFORE RETURNING **85**

    No. 1 85

    No. 16 85

    No. 17 86

    No. 18 86

    No. 25 86

    No. 29 87

    No. 30 88

    No. 39 88

    No. 43 89

    No. 50 89

POEMS OF BAGHDAD. WRITTEN AFTER RETURNING. **90**

    Thirty Days after Thirty Years 90

FROM *Sweeper of the Desert*   **93**

THE ILLUSION OF PRESENCE   **95**

    Inverted Mirror   95

    The Lost Dream   95

    Beautiful as Ever   96

    After the Return to Baghdad   96

    Mourning   97

    Open the Window   97

    Poem for Peace   98

    The Best of Words   100

    Ennui, Instant of Inspiration   100

    Ephemeral Victories   101

AN EXILE AS BIG AS A MIRAGE   **104**

    War Is Not a Lie   104

    Passionately   104

    Poem for Myself   106

FROM *Seasons of Clay*   **109**

    Embarked   111

    Defeat   112

    Shadow Figures   113

    Yesterday? I Don't Remember!   114

    Interrogation   115

    Moon of Clay   116

    No Regrets   118

FROM *Baghdad, Jerusalem,*
at the Fire's Edge   **119**

THROUGH THE STRANGER'S WINDOW   **121**

    Unexpected Worries   121

    Suffocation   121

    Always You   122

THE LAST WORD   **124**

    Nausea No Longer Has Meaning   124

    A River on Paper   126

    At the Fire's Edge   126

FROM *July Rain*   **133**

     Centred   135

     Identity   136

     The Ambience of a Port   137

     Sadness Without Confession   138

     All This   139

     Appearance of Sense   140

FROM *This Shower Comes from Another Cloud*   **141**

     Voluntary Transgression   143

     This Shower Comes from Another Cloud   145

     Baghdad, Desperately   147

     Beginning of a Ceremony   148

     As in a Dark Dream   149

     Seasons of Incertitude   150

FROM *Season of Salt*   **153**

     Mother of the Morning   155

     Homage   157

     Nebula   158

     Kite   159

FROM *Mirage*   **161**

     Obstinacy of exile . . .   163

     It's for me to interpret thirst . . .   163

     When I awake in an unclear morning . . .   164

     I wake up within you, free . . .   164

     In the drowning of the twilight . . .   164

FROM *Rebuild the Days*   **165**

     Unfinished Word   167

     Meditations   168

     Debris of Memory   169

     Low Sky   170

     Inundation   171

     Itinerary   172

Daily Bread 173

Rebuild the Days 174

FROM *Adieu, My Torturer* **177**

From 'The Crickets' Game' 179

From 'To Receive a Postcard of the Moon' 180

From 'Day of an Iraqi Exiled in Paris' 182

From 'Night Has Obscured the Paths' 184

From 'Letter to My Double' 186

From 'The Return' 187

From 'I'll Drag My Dwelling Along' 188

From 'The Man with the Wicked Laugh' 191

FROM *For You, I Dream* **193**

Notes *201*

Acknowledgements

The poet would like to thank Isabelle Lagny for her valuable collaboration with him in his translations from Arabic into French.

The translator would like to thank Isabelle Lagny for her contributions to the biographical sketch of the author presented in her Introduction; Sam Hamill for his reading of the Introduction; and Rosalind Morris for her help with the title.

I met the Iraqi poet Salah Al Hamdani, author of almost forty books in both Arabic and French, in 2003, at a poetry festival in southern France, and I was immediately struck not only by the poignancy of this exiled poet's texts but also by the beauty of his reading in French. Over our first coffee together, we discovered common interests and views on life and politics. The next step, as yet unimagined by me, would be our literary collaboration. When I suggested that his work be translated into English, I had no thought of doing it myself as I was involved in other translating projects and, in any case, had, at that time, limited experience in translating poetry. However, with his extraordinary force of character and spirit of optimism—which no doubt helped him survive his prison experience—he convinced me to try. Once I started, I found the process so gratifying that, in 2008, it resulted in the publication of my English version of his poems and narratives from 2003–2004, around the time of the invasion of Iraq.

We may ask why one should compose another selection of Salah Al Hamdani's work. My translation did introduce his powerful texts to English readers but those poems represented only a short, albeit rich, period of his writing.

/

Al Hamdani is now in his sixties and has been, since 1992, writing mainly in French. In addition, many of his Arabic texts from the 1980s and others that he, today, chooses to write in that language have been translated into French and are therefore available to translators not versed in his native tongue. It is now time to present an overview of this poet's sumptuous repertoire, to offer to English-language readers the strength and passion of Al Hamdani's poetry as it has evolved over the decades of his life.

Despite the one book that has appeared in English, Al Hamdani remains relatively unknown to a large segment of the English-language public. Before we delve into his poetry, a consideration of his life will, I believe, give us an insight into both the poet and the man.

Salah Al Hamdani's early years were not promising ones. He was a child-labourer, and unschooled but for a brief period of crudely taught night courses. At seventeen, he joined the army to support his family, but even as a soldier he continued to oppose injustice and was soon incarcerated for conspiring with a small leftist party against the ruling Bassists. It was in prison that he received his education from the other political prisoners; it was there he he learnt to write and, in time, composed his first poems. And recognized the power of the written word when, for writing a verse on the walls of his cell, a fellow prisoner warned him that he could be killed for such language. After eight months of detention and torture, he was finally released but was excluded from the army.

It was after this prison experience—unable to find work and cut off from his family who, fearing reprisals, asked him to stay away—that he began to frequent cafes where the literate youth of the Baghdad bourgeoisie gathered. He was introduced to the Arabic translations of texts by Albert Camus which went on to leave a deep impression on him.

For Al Hamdani, Camus came to represent the 'just man' who was against evil—against the Algerian revolutionaries when they killed the innocent (though he was not anti-Algerian, quite the contrary); against the French colonial policy, as well, that served to oppress the Algerian population. *The Stranger* made a powerful impression on him but it was the *Myth of Sisiphus* that was particularly influential. It was this work that Al Hamdani now acknowledges reconciled him to the idea of exile. Like Sisiphus, he was destined to undergo his own trial, the terrible one of exile. He would deal with the challenge with all his might. Reading Camus inspired him to follow what he felt was the true path regardless of the risks.

One of his recent books, *Baghdad-Jerusalem, at the Fire's Edge*, is an example of his willingness to confront risk if the path is the just one. He has written it in collaboration with an Israeli poet, Ronny Someck, of Iraqi origin. (Born in Baghdad in the same year, 1951). In the context of the ongoing Israel-Palestine conflict, collaborating with an Israeli writer has shut doors. Both the militant Arabic and Israeli communities are critical of what appears to be an acceptance either of the Israeli government's policies, on the one hand, or an embracing of Arabic extremism on the other. For Al Hamdani, sharing a publication with an Israeli poet, a Jew, who like a brother speaks his maternal Iraqi dialect, is a way of reaching across the divide between the two populations. He's willing to risk being shunned by fellow militants. It's his 'rock', his destiny to create a bridge between the two warring nations in the one way a poet can, through his writing.

Though no longer a prisoner, he remained an 'enemy' for the Saddam regime and was harassed for his political activism and union organizing. After escaping an attempted assassination, he was advised to seek exile. In 1974, sustained by his reading of Camus, Al Hamdani finally decided to leave his homeland and, with the help of some well-placed young friends (he was the author of their 'love letters'), succeeded in acquiring the papers needed to leave for Lebanon. He was determined, however, to head for France.

He made his way to Paris in 1975, not speaking a word of French, armed only with the address, unreadable to him, of a fellow Iraqi whom, after some wandering, he managed to locate. Eventually, he met a French pilot who took him under his wing and procured a student card as well as a resident card allowing him to pursue a life in France. As an adolescent, he'd been involved in folk theatre, so when he was asked what he wanted to do, theatre was an easy answer. He enrolled in theatre courses and was soon launched on a successful acting and directing career, which lasted for fifteen years. All the while he continued to militate against Saddam Hussein and to write poetry, though in solitude and with the pain of having cut his ties with his loved ones. Some of his poetry, along with narratives and short stories, was translated into French and published in *Le cimetière des oiseaux* (The Cemetery of the Birds) in 2003 (much of which was the basis for my English version that appeared in 2008.)

By 1988–89, he was well known in Paris for his active opposition to Saddam's regime, and he knew it would place his family in danger if he wrote to them. Before Al Hamdani left Baghdad, one of the few people he had informed was his mother who responded, as a mother would: 'And what will you eat there?' She perhaps never fully understood the import of his leaving—every day, she would wait on a street corner for his return. When Al Hamdani visited Baghdad in 2004, a year after the American invasion, he was warmly welcomed. But once he returned to France, his mother appeared to have accepted the idea that this son, in a sense, no longer existed for her.

The tragedy of exile is an enduring theme in his poetry. He constantly grapples with accepting the loss of his mother, of his childhood, of his homeland, of his estrangement from those once dear to him but who now have forgotten him. In 'Interrogation' from *Seasons of Clay*:

> Mother, what does the void cling to?
> The hope of seeing you again
> is a wound
> which opens
> onto an avalanche
> of words

And in *Baghdad-Jerusalem, at The Fire's Edge:*

> My mother no longer waits for me
> nor is there a turtledove
> that weeps for me

And as expressions of his thoughts on rejection and being forgotten, we read in the *Sweeper of the Desert*, in 'Poem for Peace': 'The exiled returns, like the seasons devoid of feeling, that no love awaits'. Or in 'Always You' from *Baghdad-Jerusalem*:

> Where is the inheritance of exile . . .
> and who will remember you
> in the moments of joy?

Baghdad, as one might suspect, is a metaphor for his homeland and the pain associated with its loss. Among the many allusions to the poet's native city, we read in *Beyond Pain*, in '20 July':

> with what remains of Baghdad in me
> I'll warm my winter . . .

In '2 December', we find:

> Baghdad . . . follows me like a shower . . .
> Today Baghdad is everywhere
> And in spite of the cold
> it is tracking me.

Or in *Adieu My Torturer*, in 'I'll Drag my Dwelling Along': 'Oh my Baghdad, my torment'. As the years go by, the poet comes to realize that he may never return to his beloved city. In 2010, in the *Sweeper of the Desert*, in 'Ephemeral Victories', he writes: 'I was trapped in my exile'. In 2012, he writes in *This Shower Comes from Another Cloud* in the poem with the same title: 'Exile is my homeland, not my dwelling, I'm . . . suspended over a feverish memory.'

The poet's lament on exile is profoundly affecting, but we should not neglect another crucial element of his poetry—and his life—that is fundamental and consistent: his cry against injustice and oppression, against the brutality and violence of dictators and the ravages of war. As a political prisoner, the poet has experienced the harshness of oppression. and his early poems bear traces of the physical torments he suffered that, at the time of writing, still affected him. In *Above the Table, a Sky*, from 1983, where the images are often sombre and even violent, in 'Summit of Passion', he vividly evokes this terrifying experience:

> What's in those blighted eyes?
> boils
> face of my misfortune
> on the doorstep of a nightmare . . .

and, further along,

> I've crossed the night of the cities
> men gather in my body . . . they've . . .
> smothered the day and howled:
> rape him . . .

In the later poems, the now-older poet no longer refers to his own physical suffering but to that of his fellow beings. In *The Arrogance of the Days*, from 1997, in 'The Eleventh Man', we read:

> Iraqis knock on the door.
> They're dressed in the remains of Babylonian legends
> and are assaulted by wounds from Bassora . . .
> A war comes
> a war goes, . . .
> Rebels are pursued
> rebels are killed . . . But there are only men
> and it is only Bassora that resists . . .

In *The Sweeper of the Desert*, in 'Poems for Peace', he evokes the suffering in war and the menace of tanks: 'The war has lasted many years, and all one hears is bitter moaning, as the sun sets behind the tanks.' In *Beautiful as Ever*, with

> In revolt today
> to defend life
> without madness

he is, as ever, for life with integrity but without heedless violence. In *Poem for Myself*, in the same volume, the poet exhorts others to speak up and act against violence:

> repeat after me: Passionately
> strike down silence
> cowardice.
> We need even more words and cutting acts
>   to defy the assassins
> and save our dreams from their hatred

In *Baghdad-Jerusalem*, we read in 'The Fire's Edge':

> let me thwart the traps of hatred
> and beautify the seasons of clay

And towards the end of this impressive poem dedicated to Ronny Someck: 'There's no justice by the whip.'

Although fragments of *I've Seen* appeared in Arabic as early as 1990 and 1991, the complete text was published in Arabic in 1997. A large extract was translated into French in 1993 and in 2001 the entire text was published in French by l'Harmattan. I have based my English version mainly on the extract of 1993 as it appeared in *Memory of Embers* with some changes from the 2001 version if they seemed more fitting. Though Saddam was still very much alive when Al Hamdani was writing the text in Arabic, he had a vision of his end and wondered if it wasn't a premonition or perhaps simply the expression of a profound wish. In any event, in this poem, he says:

> I've seen Saddam with his throat cut,
> and people dancing

As if in a litany, he repeats 'I've seen' again and again evoking dreadful images of Saddam's Iraq or of those who were forced into exile by him:

> . . . I've seen
> an old lady caress the clothes of a martyr . . .
> and the mutilated bodies of combatants
> spread out on paper . . .
> I've seen
> a country in flames . . .
> a newborn thrown out of a train . . .
> I've seen
> an exiled child, who resembles my son
> suffocate
> his toy is heartless, it accuses–articulates–
>   breaks-burns, swallowed by the dust . . .
> I've seen cities appear behind the tears
> of a comrade in exile . . .

fires
genocides . . .
I've seen
. . . 'the chateau of no return'
    and a faceless torturer . . .
names written on windowless walls.
. . . I've seen . . .
a people disappear into the mouth of a nightmare
spotted with blood

In the Epilogue to *I've Seen* (published in the 2001 version) we're reminded once more of an aspect fundamental to Al Hamdani's character—his defence of the weak: 'I promised myself to give refuge to trembling bodies'. We remember that, as a young boy in Baghdad, he had the reputation of being the 'protector' of the defenceless; and as a young adult, he assumed the same role in his political opposition to Saddam while in exile and as a union militant. The Epilogue is also a potent comment on the right of the exiled to share the painful destiny of those who suffer a cruel fate In Iraq. The poet still feels a part of the suffering back 'home'.

I observe myself
I peruse the newspapers
I bellow out the paralysed mornings
that are without a trace of humanity.
Yes, I possess the right to *share* with the dead.

Later he will feel the distance of the years of separation and not be sure about having the same rights as those who are back home and suffering.

In *Adieu, My Torturer*, one of his last books, Al Hamdani faces the torturer of his youth: 'the illusions of my youth were as frail as one of my miserable days'. The pain of exile is ever present: 'existence in the rotten waters of separation

... years consumed far from the faces of loved ones' but also the realization, as a mature poet, that he must transcend it and forge a new life. 'O Baghdad, I no longer expect anything of you . . . no longer dream of a return of that far-off time . . . I'm going to close my writing on that city and its inhabitants. I'll offer a new horizon to my exile'. Yet, in spite of his loss of homeland, of his past, he remains true to himself: 'I am stripped of everything except my spirit of revolt.'

In his work from 2015, *For You, I Dream*, dedicated to his newborn granddaughter, we see him return to the incantatory style of *I've Seen*. Permeated by thoughts of his past suffering and the shadows of his never-ending exile, his laments as well as his aspirations are put into the hands of the infant, *Lou*, the incarnation of the future. In his dedication to his granddaughter, we see the poet's commitment to a new life in his adopted land of France.

In this anthology of Salah Al Hamdani's work that spans decades, from 1983 to 2015, the theme of exile is never far from his thoughts. Baghdad, the place of his birth and childhood, is ubiquitous and again and again we find images of palms, dunes, mirages, sands and deserts. Yet, in the trajectory of his exile, changes over the years are inevitable. The young poet dreams of return; the older, wiser poet, recently a grandfather, has achieved the understanding that comes with age and experience—the realization that there is no home to which he can return. As he writes in *Mirage*:

I become my own country
a cemetery of dreams

He must, after all the years of exile, assume his destiny in France:

If Baghdad gave birth to me
France made me a man' (*Season of Salt*).

He remains a poet of exile. The wound will stay with him for ever, but his life and his continuing rage, his 'spirit of revolt', confronting injustice and cruelty will be in the here and now, in France.

A Note on the Poems

Salah Al Hamdani has written almost forty books of poetry and narratives. In this volume, the reader will find a selection from 1983 to 2015, giving an overview of the poet's work for more than thirty years. Some of the books I've chosen were written in Arabic and then translated into French. Others the poet wrote in French, first in collaboration with Elizabeth Brunet Sancho and, later, with Isabelle Lagny. In all cases, I have translated from the French version, usually from the second edition where it exists.

I have selected from the following volumes:

Originally written in Arabic and then translated into French:

- *Over the Table, a Sky* (*Au-dessus de la table, un ciel*)—in Arabic, 1983; in French 1988 (2nd edition, 2000).
- *Memory of Embers* (*Mémoire de braise*)—in Arabic, 1986; in French, 1993.
- *I've Seen* (*J'ai vu*)—complete Arabic version, 1997; selections in French, 1993; complete French version, 2001.
- *Arrogance of the Days* (*L'Arrogance des jours*)—in Arabic, 1996; in French, 1997.
- *Baghdad-Jerusalem, at the Fire's Edge* (*Bagdad-Jérusalem, à la lisière de l'incendie*)—trilingual edition (Arabic, French and Hebrew) with Ronny Someck, 2012.

Originally written in French:

- *What Remains of Light* (*Ce qui reste de lumière*)—1999
- *Beyond Pain* (*Au large de douleur*)—2000

- *The Open Sky of Baghdad* (*Bagdad à ciel ouvet*)—2006
- *Sweeper of the Desert* (*Le balayeur du désert*)—2010
- *Rebuild the Days* (*Rebâtir les jours*)—2013. A compilation of the following limited art editions that appeared between 2010 and 2012, with the inclusion of a final section, *Rebuild the Days* from 2012.

    'July Rain' (*Pluie de juillet*)

    'This Shower Comes from Another Cloud' (*Cette averse vient d'un autre nuage*)

    'Season of Salt' (*Saison de sel*)

    'Mirages' (*Mirages*)

    'For You, I Dream' (*Je te rêve*)—2015

I should note that, in 2008, Curbstone Press published *Baghdad Mon Amour*, my English translation of poems and narratives from Al Hamdani's *The Cemetery of the Birds* (*Le cimetière des oiseaux*) and his memoir, *The Return to Baghdad* (*Le retour à Bagdad*, 2004).

One poem ('Thirty Days After Thirty Years') from *Baghdad Mon Amour*, written after Al Hamdani's return to Baghdad, has been included in this volume.

*

Sometimes I have left out a line or two of the poems if I felt doing so was appropriate for the English and did not detract from the original intent of the work. All such liberties have been taken in consultation with the poet.

Sonia Alland

FROM
Above the Table, a Sky

Exit

They enter, the mirror and the veil
faces torn
and men, nameless
she returns,
the snow . . .
then the light becomes bleak
cowardly
the night howls outside
cold
and the shadow wanders
the wall collapses

And she returns, my mother, with her shawl
heavy with distance

There it is, Baghdad, the ancient one
pregnant
and I, bald inside,
I enter the air, tubercular,
and the skylark dies,
in the water the plague is born
they cut the sea's throat,
calls from sailors
the sky is sterile
sleep has only one eye
I pour
break among the splinters of glass
I howl

my feet are swollen
and in my body frontiers are dying
I vomit, a wounded dream
and become the far off
and in the mirror's face
weeping eye of an old witch
falling
head gnawed by moths
and a sodden owl.

Summit of Passion

What's in those blighted eyes?
boils
face of my misfortune
on the doorstep of a nightmare
a man, a dream,
humid
a worn rope
I feel the heat
       heat
chance/day-time dream
for here men are born ephemeral
I've crossed the night of the cities,
men gather in my body
sexless, not looking
they've erased the colours
smothered the day and howled:
rape-him
I smile maliciously/owl of the sea
stop short the flames of beings
their wives
the women cry out:
kill him, time flies
flight of bats from childhood
from the ulcer's fissure
and the blood trembles
my body is a battlefield
for assaulting defeated people
respiration/rock

phantoms stone me
I'm an alien crow
a gnome who harvests the bitter soul
and plants swings in the street
where white men hang grotesquely
as if issued from green water

and the harmful dead arise.

FROM
Memory of Embers

To those close to me here and in Iraq,
who knew how to leave embers burning in my memory

Saddam
It's time that the dead
devour your heart!!

The First Day

I have only one wish,
to see my mother
among those rocks
emerging from the sand and the waves
that prowl on the beach
before dying.

The Fourth Day

The facades of the houses have not changed,
the terraces look the same as well
except a woman, obese, who undresses
shameless.
Before the Fakhati of adolescence
she takes off her memories,
still impregnated with war,
hangs them on the rope of isolation,
opposite a window in ruins,
on the sidewalk of expectation.

The mailman smiles.

The Sixteenth Day

. . .

My solitude
is like those bizarre creatures
that spring out of the bowels of the sea,
in the eyes of a child who wakes in me,
with his *desdasha* and his runny nose.
He writes in me, shakes the dust from the cities,
protests,
cries out in the consumptive mornings,
that are roused
in out-of-the-way corners of cemeteries,
from the victims of the war
stacked in the spirit.

Oh, mother,
that child can no longer bear the absence of the palms.

The Twenty-Ninth Day

. . .

The morning is calm
like a dog sleeping near a hunter.

Some kids, out of breath, approached us
telling us to look at the horizon.

The first one said:
'It's a storm, muzzled for ages.
It can breathe now.'

The second one said:
'No . . . I think it's rain, prisoner of a cloud,
that will flow into the earth's mouth.

It's been eating the gravel, the dust and men for years,
now it's dying in the bowels of a peasant,
who lives beyond the mountains and feeds on serpents.'
But I,
I didn't listen to what they were saying,
I knew that the tempest,
was only the voices
of the innocent dead,
the cries of a woman
and of an orphan who came to visit me
so that I'd cut the sea's neck
and the distance.
With the blood of God, I water the nostalgia of childhood,
I saddle my heart, martyred by the neighing of the twilight,
    and set out for Iraq.

Homage

I wish I were a partisan returning from war,
one leg amputated.
The women from the quarter would welcome me
with *youyous* and grains of rice.
My mother would kiss me and wipe the sweat from my
forehead,
She'd chase away the flies
buzzing around my meal,
blow into my hot soup,
tell me about the festivals
and the men who were returning.

She'd laugh at my stories,
and, when she was alone,
she would weep over my lost leg.

Story

In the street where I live,
from time to time
a mule passes by, dragging a cart.
The cart pulls a dog,
the dog barks at my window.
Baghdad stalks in my room.

From *I've Seen*

I've seen
gatherings bound to memory
and skylarks burdened with bundles
of sadness,
hiding under the mound of coats
from broken soldiers . . .

. . . I've seen
ulcerated wounds that creep and swallow Baghdad . . .
. . . I saw myself in a mirror,
saw abandoned poets in the rain,
coats, trains, parachutes,
disquiet and insomnia . . .

. . . I've seen my mother
under the moonlight of Norouz
curved in her shawl,
birds' wings,
dates torn by bullets from the war,
the homeland assassinated
vows and pain suffocated in a morning . . .

. . . I've seen Saddam with his throat cut,
and people dancing
the dance 'Betrayal'
and die.

. . . I've seen
an old lady caress the clothes of a martyr,
conversing with the embers,
a writer lost among the generations and the smiles
of women whipped by the law of Gods,
who polish the boots of soldiers.
Potential lost in old newspapers
and the mutilated bodies of combatants
spread out on paper.

I've seen
a sailor sobbing on the sidewalk of a port,
a priest jump from the roof of a church,
and a bearded fisherman with the sea
and the sun behind him
on his boat
heading into the void.

I've seen
a peasant exhibit his wife to guests
who don't know the language of hunger
and a mariner in the darkness,
hit his head against an abandoned lighthouse,
and soldiers who hang their age on naked walls,
proud in the emptiness.

My curses drown the calendar of 1987
the war IRAK-IRAN is in its seventh year.

I've seen
poems and books by exiled poets,
scattered in a cemetery of days,
words by painters and politicians
chased by dogs.

I've seen
a country in flames, newspapers read upside down,
mercenaries gathering at a bloody frontier,
a newborn thrown out of a train,
and a woman open a cloud discreetly,
       laughing at a tomb.

. . . I've seen
an exiled child, who resembles my son,
suffocate,
his toy is heartless, it accuses–articulates–
              breaks–burns, swallowed by the dust.

Iraq is a word violated in the language of Baathists
. . .
I've seen
poets praise famine, anemic children,
praise the sand, the palms and the bridges.
Their dreams, a memory of regrets and calamity,
claws planted in the arteries of the soul.
And I, oh Iraq, I'm like a heart that burns,
embers of words.

I've seen cities appear behind the tears
of a comrade in exile,
who draws stars, black planets
and moons in mourning,
neither sea, nor the Euphrates, nor return, fire,
fires,
genocides.

I've seen,
. . . 'the chateau of no return' and a faceless torturer,
closed valises, forgotten seasons,
sleeping among the folds of a ragged shirt,

unbearable odour,
names written on windowless walls.

. . . I've seen,
a fish burn in water,
a peasant not return to his fields
pebbles, stones, ruins,
alleys empty of children's laughter,
a top abandoned in the gutter
a cloud that flees the open space.

. . . I've seen,
the dead celebrate the living,
a people swallowed by its history,
a homeland lose itself in a prayer,
a people disappear into the mouth of a nightmare
spotted with blood,
curses fly up from an illuminated page
of the uprising of March.

Epilogue

What does the ephemeral life of man mean?

The flight of a bird
that emerges from a rain-soaked notebook
left on the roof of a house.
It carries in its beak the language of revolt
and, across the seas,
sets it down on a tomb extended over the void.

I promised myself to give refuge to trembling bodies,
to derive from the deluge
winter's isolation.

I'll sing for the absent
and for those who leave for the palms spotted with blood.
I'll be there for the burial of the tyrant.

Never again will I fear
the fall of a cloud in a glass,
or the wind in an empty box.
Humiliation still rots in memory.

Friend, what limits fear?
Is it to take a hammer to break a mirror?
Is it to keep watch in the street?
This corridor is empty,
and the fragments of mirror no longer reflect my virility,
but rather the disquiet of growing old,
and an intense thirst for the foolishness of childhood.
Then what limits fear?
Is it to pursue the words
that evoke the return?

Is it to seize a stick and the instant
to track down the blood of the dead,
to reconstruct language?
Is it to stab insomnia,
to take hold of the frontiers
and fasten the Tigris and the Euphrates
to impede their fleeing from Iraq?

. . .

I observe myself,
I peruse the newspapers,
I bellow out the paralysed mornings
that lack any trace of humanity.

Yes, I possess the right to *share* with the dead,
who have traversed long distances.

. . .

Yes, you, the exiled
you possess the right to *share* your crumbs,
shroud of solitude between your teeth.
You, who decipher your assassination
in the lines of news

Yes
To you the right to dream
of a return among men.

Yes
To you, the earth.
To you, the joy.
To you, the dream.

Yes
you the despoilt,
to you the right to witness the affliction of the fascists,
each one pinned to his tomb.

Letter
My son

Today, between the birds of misfortune
and the men of shame,
between the butchers of children and those of liberty,
the homeland is the beginning and the end of the frontiers
of tombs.

You will not open the door
nor jump the wall,
Iraq is the cemetery of history.
Today, my son,
the Iraqi is a walking tomb,
a growing cancer.

Tomorrow, my son,
after the earth of your ancestors has become
a grave for Saddam,
you'll take dust for memory
and storks for witnesses,
you'll sit next to a heart,
attached to the roots of a beating palm tree,
you'll eat the fruit of the date palms
and the voice of a little girl will cry out,
that their pits are her blood.
You'll thirst for the Euphrates,
you'll drink mouthfuls of its water,
you'll rub out your face with the blood of the victims
of an ordinary day.
There where you'll step,
you'll feel the earth move,
you'll understand then,
that the dead want to recapture the light.
The grave is an eye,
rags become a shroud,
and the skin of the starved dead
is the banner for the generation of genocide.

My son,
in your soul
their number decays
and in your blood they struggle
to see life again.

After 6840 Days of Exile

My days no longer have that blind necessity
of structuring obsolete words,
on the body of the river,
with waves of corpses
cloisonné in their own flesh.

Close the door on history,
hunt it down!
Close windows and roads.
Pin dreams to the children's cemetery.

What, at present, can my exile harvest.
after becoming the crossroad
of doubt, shame and misfortune,
if it's not the guilt of having departed?

The Arrogance of the Days

The Second Man

At times you stab the sea
at times you drown in forgetfulness
at times you contemplate nothingness
and at times you want to wake up
but your soul has departed.

The Third Man

Don't say:
I know nothing of men's sadness
I know nothing of those laments
and charred words
I know nothing of the solitude
that grows like cemeteries of thistles
in the eyes of the condemned.

You shouldn't say:
I know nothing of the road
where the stories of my ancestors are buried
as you turn away
from the map
that traces the blood.

The Fourth Man

From birth to exile
and from exile to exile

From patience to forgetfulness
and from the tomb to damnation

Let's go!

And the one who has
a touch of wisdom
let him light the way

The Eleventh Man
For Al Saggar

In me
the assassin is the victim
but he who looks on, who is he?

At times I gather neglected tears
that cover the pallor of the seasons.
They run in the hallways of sand
unknown to the cities' inhabitants.

At times I plant some rain-wind
and a few shy silences.

As night slips by
you unfold your memory
and you hunt for words
in the wee hours of the morning.
A child comes,

a child dies.
Iraqis knock on the door.
They're dressed in the remains of Babylonian legends
and are assaulted by wounds from Bassora.
They dig on a far-off moon
a moon unknown by the horizon.

A war comes,
a war goes.

And you, you keep company
with your Sufism.

Lines, lines
sadness, lines
walls-colours
lines-clay.
Features of a riverbank
undamaged by these fragments?
By chance the travelling star ignites.
You slice it in two
hoping that in the mirror
an oasis springs up
from your icy face.

Tell me then,
what has become of the evenings
in El Ashar?

Rebels are pursued,
rebels are killed.

But there are only men
and it is only Bassora that resists
and flourishes in your hands.

For it is you who has tattooed the autumn leaves
and scattered them among the echoes
of solitary streams of the exiled.

Nostalgia never dies
neither does your wakefulness
and your Bassora, Saggar,
resounds nowhere else but in our soul.

The Seventeenth Man

Our homeland carried us away
in threadbare valises.
Then it dispersed us among the countries,
like an adventurer
who passes through each station
spitting mirrors
ink,
death,
and men with tubercular wings.

Baghdad

From the balcony of old age
one sees
at each arrival of the rain
a man of clouds
chained to the weeping seasons.

One day I'll come
like a sudden shower
a flurry of larks
that lands on the roof of your house.

Don't be miserly,
open the window.

For at the height of dawn,
I'll tell you about the drama of exile,
then,
I'll feast on my wings
to cease my flying.

The Tenth Day

For Jawad Bashara
After 14 years.

It's that night
late,
memory of defeat
of a day that was met
then abandoned on the platform of exile
a fugitive platform in valises
where dead days pile up.
That day penetrates time,
late, and buries itself,
with wilted wings
in my breast
inflamed with the odour of villages
where sputter the sparks of the awakening
of humid stars
still battered
oozing the pain of my childhood wounds,
those that protest the fables of paradise,
protest the walls.
Then,
fingers extend,
and, as always, clean the shelves
where dusk was sleeping.
Lips breathe out.
Then,
the hand takes the old photo,
and the head is in the mirror.
Thus I see him crouching in the flames
with the past and his rusty smile.
He cries
like a wind that spreads the shivering

of infirm bodies
dead yesterday, near the rocks
dying rocks.
I see him seated,
standing,
but always the victim of fear
like a virgin
running
in a narrow corridor
that opens onto traceless sand.
And once again the lips breathe out.
And for the millionth time
fly away the voice,
the soul,
the smile,
and the emptiness.

The Eleventh Day

To my father, once again

This impoverished day,
the dawn of the hearth
drowned by our neighbour's tears
and my spirit, father,
are over forty years old.

In the soul of the days,
I appear
like an exile.
An exile who embraces Iraq
pulverizes mornings,
cages
and seasons.

First Look

My children,
let's never forget
between the massacre
and the insanity of illusion
there was a line of tombs.

And that at present
between fidelity
and betrayal
the years pile up in the howling of the wind
on the hill of isolation.

Second Look

I entered a mirror
far from the eyes of assassins.
Secretly I opened it:
Baghdad was my love
and my curse.

Fourth Look

But why do the sons of exile draw only
the sorrow of stars
and the mourning of planets?
And why
in the separation

does my boy draw
neither sea
nor trees,
nor cities in colour?

Behind his tears
could there be only
burning,
fire
and massacre?

Seventh Look

I remember the rattle in the Bedouins' throats
as they sang
I remember the village women's arms
the eclipse in the south
the shanty towns,
and the death camps
with hands that sifted water
to wash that sand.

Twelfth Look

Red Mourning

At the summit of my cell
I gouge a hole
and the winged light of hope escapes
from my ailing nostalgia.
Then sorrow rushes in
and envelops the remnants.
I know,
no longer can my thoughts appease the spirit.
And even the beating of my heart

no longer leaves a shadow on dawn's reflection
for this light that mourns
cries out in me at every sunset
up to the ending of the day.

I'm like a book abandoned at childhood,
mildewing on the shelf of adulthood.
Nothing,
not even a skylight
will allow my escape.

Incessantly I fill my throat
with a fluttering of words,
with remains
of nocturnal darkness.

Incessantly I load my throat
with morning light
and dry my seasons on the barbed wire of the city.

Things were like that
or perhaps they weren't
or they may have been both.

One could say
that the palms have come to me.
They knock at the door of my absence
and now doze on the steps of ancient Baghdad.

What has happened, my Iraq?
Your tombs resemble hunchbacked wings
shaped by the wind of the dead
who pound on my casement each night
and leave tattoos of blood on the eyes of my past.

Here is my hand stretched out that strikes.
It is submerged in history.
Here is my hand.

I look at it still
and shake my blood
like a banner
for the caravans about to leave this dark cell.

If I look again,
my being is nothing more than a breast
for the newborns over there
who cry endlessly.

And over there the dead fall
from forgetfulness
out of the tears
of a god

The Beacon of Makeshift Houses

Naked
the walls are naked
and the frames.

Childhood gone,
I ride the wreckage of my maturity,
and the clinging sweat of anguish
menaces.

I was the beacon of the marsh-land gondolas
and the breath of the date palms,
bloodied now by nausea.

So I pluck the instants
I tear out sorrow
and the palm trees.
Man of the south
I open my arms
to the horrors of civilization.
And I cadence the years
vein
by vein.

I name the names,
the source of my nightmares,
bloodied wings.
And my mouth muzzled by torment

chews the cadavers of the impossible
the odour of the night,
and the dead rain.

I swallow the vanity
of my wounds
moulded into a frame
chagrin of the orphan
of the stranger, of the untouchable.
And my face fissured
I blend with
the floating cadavers
the decay.

Naked,
I am

and the marshes

The City of Sand

For Ariane

In the city of sand
there's a body
anchored to the horses of wind,
close upon the temple of time
where birds read
to the stars
born from fields of blue.
You know
the fields that sleep
since days gone by
in the heart of a gold fish.

In the city of sand
there's someone
who writes the history of silence
on the shores of the river
and the memory of water
perched on the leaves
of imaginary trees.

You know
where there's neither crow
nor cawing
that watch over the solitude of our nights.

In the city of sand
there are one thousand, nine hundred and ninety-seven
skies,
things are born and die,
like books.

In the city of sand
I'm the keeper of the palms
and the labourer of light,
you'll be the queen
of the moths
at my awakening.

In the city of sand
do you see those bodies
grown old
reading the absence of lost days
in the morning air
of your eyes
honey and wings of crystal?

In the city of sand
history slumbers,
the days breathe slowly
and time flowers
at the hand of a man
who paints the stars,
wind that revives
the smile in your impudent eyes.

A Homeland

In your body
the odour of drowned islands
defeat
without men, without time.
Seas that I fear
and a vagabond tomb
where I look for my face.

In me
I open the windows
and the plague rushes in
a riot of horses.

For in your body
a lost boy
adorns himself with rings of death.
And men come from over there
without a name
without a story.
They remove their skin
forgotten streets
and in shivering disquiet
doze
on my shoulders.

The Necrologist

For Ghanem Hamdoun

On the skin
old traces
of abandoned corridors
and tired cawing.
I ride winter's path,
I curl up in the sequels of wounds
I wilt in my overcoat.

My fingers hold
my heart, blood cake for vagabonds
lying in my mother's memory.

I'm an amputated finger
that fidgets on paper
where I break,
like a riding-whip
I slash my throat
I shatter
I'm the apostle of death.
In my flesh
are crucified
ruined villages
waiting peasants
a white obscurity
and a miserable inn
for the midnight poet.

In the dust of my eyes
villages for burning
and men drugged
with the tuberculosis of children.
Cyclone.

I'm a crippled sailor
hidden behind a broken mirror
I've neither dagger
nor tobacco.
I offer an elegy to the earth
and veils, with uneasy cities,
take flight.

I penetrate
room by room
gallery by gallery
for the sun withdraws to die.

I tie myself
to water, the flesh of clay
black scar
mirror, without a face
without wrinkles
assassinated by solitude.
For the anguish that warms me
will not dissipate chagrin over Iraq
and my blood is a butterfly
snared in the silvery air.

I penetrate
I row on the arch of evil
with bones that are hollow.
And the calamities of strangers
are a cemetery of rain,
and the feverish horses,
a flood
that founders in the dryness
of a raging panic.

And still, behind eyelids,
those dead wings.

FROM
What Remains of Light

For Alya

Who Makes the Wind Blow?

The streets I no longer remember
the stork dying on the page
its beak
thirst for light
the wind
and this window ajar
open to the pain
of an indefinable life.

Time fades away
far off
over there
Father, tell me
again.

A Touch of Light

To sing the sea in an inkwell
step swiftly on a white page
run early on the banks of an imaginary river
and unfold one's skin in the tempest of days.
Mirage of tombs
temple of clay
beating of the heart on the sand
light.

I know the one who takes care of the dust
and the one the dust cares for.
Yet,
I've nothing to do
with the origin of silence
and this city closes late,
so late on my life.

Words Have Bodies

This first word in me,
like a lion
vanquished by serpents.
Other words will come
and I'll be a horseman
who straddles the shadows
flying into the rift of the day.

This second word in you,
far off.
And I see myself lost
in a world
that has the odour of men's cries.

This third word in her,
a lament.
And in the mirror's distance
her prayers come to me
like palm trees in trance
born on the spine of the sky.

And the God
Yes.
In your eyes
I see a God that greets me.
In me
you count the words,
count the names and the dead.

You enfold me
though my heart is devoured
by the hyenas of memory.

This fourth word in her
still
and my boat knows nothing of her shores.

I'll remain perhaps
the one who accepts losing
to the sabre of your absence.

This fifth word
I cry it out again

and my insomnia
leaves a fissure in the sea.

Near Withered Time

Allow me
as dusk descends
to gasp the names of strangers.
And the wall of regret grinds
with the gesture of the ploughman
under the devastated sky.

Allow me
to mingle our souls
with the destiny of cemeteries.

Allow me
to receive the call of unknown islands
and the expectation of the shipwrecked.

Allow me
to abandon myself to our childhood
and to dreams of the future.

Assuredly I'll be the one
who bites the days' edge
and makes the time suffer.

A Monday Afternoon

Pulling the curtain on things,
those things we'd never mentioned,
my little sun gathered in a humid and lazy lake,
blending with the instants.
From high on your body, I could see the sea,
the accent of an ancient temple and the laughter of
horses.

Your eyes guided me towards an old sailor
who drew me to the shore
in a boat of buffoons.

Over there
along side your body soaked with the froth of stars,
you bound me once again
with the beating of your dawn,
and I,
I showed you the island of glass.

Grave-Digger

I was a sabre that stabbed the mirage of the steppes
and my dwelling place was nostalgia.

Grave-digger!
look at this little shower in me
that sweeps down the hill.
Shake the sleep of this humanity from my body.

Then I'll bury cities and the thirst of the desert,
I'll become a path punctuated by canyons.
Man of fire
Man of snow
in my coat the writings dream of an encounter
with time past
with fields of wheat
with hunched-back flowers.

Grave-digger!
Man is ready to believe in the devil
and I, look at me,
an exile!
A charred hand
that learnt to write alone in the soul of fountains.

Look grave-digger
how they hasten
one behind the other, one glued to the other
under the light of the clouds.

Madness,
collect what remains of this body
and follow me
like a black
who tans the day with his skin.

You say the words of a poet are a cancer.
But from his silence emerges a strange traveller,
always at the place where roads cross.

Then do not depict me in the grave,
my death refuses your wreath of roses.

And if it happens,
grave-digger,
that my child weeps far from me
in the sobbing of the night,
may the earth become flat
and the sky be without space.

Everything Passes

To my friend, Frédéric Guillaumond

Of that river, over there,
the water bitter with memories
where the nights of my childhood
plunge one after the other
to finish in the clarity of the seasons,

only the red clay
and its moon
remain in me
anchored to the cemetery of the days.

In that alley, over there,
a God
a vault, a prayer?
And for the mother who grieves in a mirror,
where is the mirror?

At the end of those few strings clinging to the sun
were there roofs that still embraced the sky?

And in that boat in the midst of the fields
perfumed with spices
where are the little bodies
that ran after wrinkles of age
like stars
lost in the void of a mirage?

My fate has known all of men's wars
the awakening of the shepherd
and the fish who thrashes on the page of sand.

You see, on the terrace of the night,
I alone am vanquished.

Everything passes, my friend
the silver moon
and the handkerchief starred with our weeping.

Everything passes,
children without tenderness
deserted piers, newspaper vendors,
and even soldiers who have betrayed.

In the breath of the survivors,
there are only tears.

In the language of my river,
no one waits for me
save a few black flowers
and a future already in mourning.

Still, you see,
what now belongs to me
what enlivens my days
are your questions
like the swelling of the sea.

Act

I've ceased dying for the days passed by
and for the dead time on paper.

I've taught my hands to erase the mirror
the lamp behind the curtains
and the winter strolling on the roof
with your image.
Where is the wind?

Very late, once again,
I want to trace another light
a torrent of mornings
where my nights dance only for you.

Assembling

I've closed down the nights. Memories elude me. When the wind calls, I raise my hand. Wind, tell me: where is my childhood? Then the echo of the past answers: detach an arm from my body and shake it towards the sun. Stop dreaming of your return. Not a face, not a name comes back. Only the echo. The mirror of sand is a thirsty sea. And the retreat of the Bedouin, its happiness. A few donkey brays, some camel cries and a spot of shadow for sleeping at midday. A little tobacco and some ground coffee, and a woman who sweeps the desert.

Man is the assassin and his victim
and a mouth nourished with hate
will never know a smile.

Before, the window was a hole in the wall, and the space between the bedrooms couldn't contain the moon. The house was no more than a little silence, a bit of sun and a little rain facing the virgins who wait for the sand to swirl before they weep.

The word *mourning* starts at birth. And calamities, in the moans of the mother, like a stormy sunrise. So you, the source of my memory's pain, how can you expect me not to call you for help?

My window is latched open to the ceiling today. It attracts the fugitive birds of these poems, attracts the night wolves that attract the plague, and Baghdad. But my wound refuses to heal and robs me of peace.

Whether it be early in the morning or late in the evening, there are those who slit the cow's throat and those who milk her. My mother is the one who sows rice inside the house of bricks and then awaits the coming of the rain.

The clouds have not visited her, not even the guests invited to the betrothal. The rice has not grown.

But tell me why did my mother always cry at the coming of the evening?

And why the does boy, who ripped up flowers in the calm of a spring morning, run through gardens tearing off butterfly wings?

Give Back My Waiting

To the one who possesses the thickness of the shadow,
to the one who flits about endlessly
like the mirage of butterflies in an album
and makes my throat ache,
to her I've abandoned my lamp
and the air of distant forests.

And we go round together
each having a turn with her
like those horses who lose their balance
in a field of words.

Is it you
who has assassinated the banished one?
or is it the guardian of your sad dreams
who has closed the door to my sleep
and thrust my salvation
towards the sky and its seasons of lies?
What have you done with the keys to the wind?
What have you done with the door
and our two bodies, drunk, in the mirror?

No my love
don't return the mockery of the past to me
still too close
to the target of my vanquished days.

I wait for you then
and, round about, all becomes calm
with our summer's rain.

Do you know the man strangled by waiting
behind the prairie hedges?
Was it only me
or perhaps your god
who cast the anchor into my body
this boat abandoned by men?

Without you
things are tasteless but in place
and my sailboat-heart
a coffin in a text.

I'm going to set each thing in its spot
the tree
the bird
the tears of the wind on the bench of the forgotten
and my secrets
leaning as always over the riverbanks of your dreams.

Render to each thing its expectations
like the storm over the haven of your body.

And for your eyes that can no longer bear my promises
I'll resuscitate
what was erased by the sand.

The Memory of Clay

They forged my absence,
I, the most ancient of the temples of misfortune.

Like a mirage of winged cattle
my wounded seasons collide
and from those days that follow,
dreams are born broken
on a lost cloud
near a riverbank of reverie.

Those are my thoughts,
suspended in the movement
of a hapless body, weary,
listless from a barren revolt.

A body consoled,
tattooed after those fearful days
and the bluntness of my candour
that opens onto an endless winter.

I am a sky travelling to other places
where my earth has no age.

I count the embers,
harvest the breath of dust.
And the silence,
passion of a lake from elsewhere,
keeps watch over my memory, despondent
from absence.

Neighing Towards Baghdad

I want to change these wilted mornings
change this vase,
and the road leading back to your tomb.

I want to change the sun's place,
to fire on this night that fixes its eyes on me.

I want to pluck out my black star,
roll, trample, fling,
then wrest the joy from my lost days.

Nail a window in place of my face
so that the heart of that betrayed boy
and the deceiving seasons
can breathe inside the walls.

I want to punish the chains, the memories,
the futile emotion
and the truth of virtue.

I'll no longer say:
ennui, that strange mariner.

I want to seize my flotilla of sand,
my paper horse,
my soldiers in rags,
and with fireworks mark your defeat.

I want to hear my neighing towards Baghdad,
when the moon smells good in the eyes of my children.

Those are my reasons for being, my madness
and my wounds.

I want to cherish their youth,
as one hugs a proud palm tree,
in a dawn laboured by storms.

Then I'll abort the years to celebrate your funeral.

Remember,
my days are like the ink of memory,
They take me back always
to the lonely path of mourning.

Still

You and this page,
smiling at times
despite the dagger.

Still the sand
still this question
full of the dead and the disappeared.

If you only knew!
The disappeared,
my stars,
these flowers turned into coal,
dead now,
and yet!

Destiny

Only now
I'll close my book on the war.
Put away the guns,
the song of tanks.
I'll close the tombs,
close my notebook on time.
The Euphrates is far away,
as far as the distress of youth.

Who will still love me
in my little field of the dead?
Who will wait for me with my foolishness?
You perhaps,
or those little spots of sun attached with mockery
on the walls of age?

And destiny
resembles those livelong nights
forgotten in the inkwell.

One shouldn't say: *Time stands still.*
Say rather: *It flies.*

Yet, here is the chalk for rebellion.
A woman the colour of water,
of flesh
and a silver moon
prostituting itself late into my night.

Then there are her eyes
the cast of her eyes.

FROM
Beyond Pain

*For my children Kermel, Salah, Anissa and Inès
and Alya, my beloved*

5 January

Alone

My head opposing what survives
I track down the lie of this unbearable life
then, the rage of things
cage,
children in a notebook
cold coffee
smile on an unknown face
dreams wrinkled in a sheet
a city in mourning . . . and another wall.

Standing, facing this tide of absences
I weave my thirst, your captive
I stumble over my nights
and I slip on my gestures in disorder
to reach those of the palms.

7 January

From my room, tonight
I grow a palm tree
in whose shelter I quench my thirst.
I draw a sun
that doesn't warm me
and gather grains of sand
resembling my childhood tears.

Thus
I'll follow men
without knowing their fate
and cry my life out to you
even from its ruins.

2 March

As high as the night
far from your eyes
late
like an ancient guard of hope
I gather the days remaining to me
and I fill my hands with your face.

With you only,
confronting my body
without roots
a windmill of time
an hour glass

from which life falls
like a sudden shower.

8 March

Today
my dwelling is a refuge of stars
and of walls tattooed by my voice.
I came into the world gazing at a palm,
and above my table, I've invented a horizon
for executed comrades.

Today
I write my life on an empty chessboard
I surround myself with strings of metal
a little wind and dead ink.

In my vast mirror,
I'll let enter
only those drowned by words
and the flight of birds announcing the deluge.

12 March

From the far reaches of my long night
distance erases our thoughts
and light thickens
on the face of things
like dust that envelops my farewells.

At the end of each day
I carry the Euphrates up to my room
and the punishment of exile spreads
like smoke from a battle
into the drifts of my tranquillity.

7 April

Do not open the window
for I'm the nightfall that is taking flight.

Ever in the shadow of the mirror,
facing your dream, powerless
I approach you with unsure steps
and, weary, turn away.

I say:
One should not plunge one's hands
into an exile's story
when one is so often condemned
to harvest memory's storm.

28 June

I've drawn a moon over my table
traced streams in my room
ploughed sweat into your hills
decapitated time
erased words
heavier than tears.

And to see you
        I've even misplaced in my flesh
a country, poor and desolate.

30 June

Now, all must disappear.
This miserable fourth floor,
my neighbour,
my memories, Baghdad
and even my body.
Naked,
my body still wet with its illusions
I stand behind the curtains of my room
watching for the sunrise with a gesture, unexpected
a look, inarticulate, that turns back
calmly crossing the morning
to see how, over there,
the earth embraces
the assassinated.

3 July

One of your desires is limitless.
It sweeps away death and this ephemeral life
like my naked breath
on your skin.

Yet everything, for men, must be redone.
I've fashioned a city
surrounded by hills of sand and rain.
And on the asphalt in the deep of winter
I've made a mirage rise up.
For you, I've become
a roof
and for your body, a refuge.

Today there is no art
no poems,
only your leaving
and the beating of my heart.

20 July

Because I saw you when the rain began to fall
I think sometimes my train has returned.

With what remains of Baghdad in me
I'll warm my winter
and bore into time to see its face.

Baghdad resembles me.
I turn towards its mirage
under the watch of an imaginary river.

By the glow of the night
I clasp the wounded wings of the dawn
and I strike off the days.

25 July

Still July bedding down with the mildew of its past. What is secret in a season without odour, without trace of my bare feet?

One night, I left Baghdad with no address. I heard the beating of the river. Lying on its back, it was breathing, asleep. In the morning, under the new moon steeped in my mother's eyes, I understood the river was dying.

Who today will shake off the sadness and the issue of my gesture?

Your god knows nothing of the refuge of poets and its orphaned islands, and I, I despise the paths in the cemetery of exile. Do then what you will with my love, but don't let it fade away.

In this month of July, I'm like a mother who sees her child drowning.

26 August, Jeu Les Bois

The silence of expectation
that drawn-out ruse against chance
will carry me inevitably towards the end
to dig over there
a hole in the wind.

Tell me,
who else but you will help me unravel
what remains of the days,
will deliver me from the barbed-wired dreams
where exile is born ?

With you
I wanted the river to accompany my steps,
the naked page to speak with my voice,
and the wind to sculpt your cry.

Sad wrinkles against those of the night
under the trampling of the seasons,

and soon the cold
and the long winter
of this exile.

12 November

I no longer resist the call of the wind.
I, the ant, with my ant anger,
I give you this day free of hail,
this corner of the morning where the stork is dying.

The spirit burns at the feast for the dead,
the city is deserted
and I am cold.

1 December

Winter river,
a gesture without violence on the facade of a deceptive
peace
my days bed down on the frost.

What to say
and how to harvest words
and every language in your hands is a doubt,
and every language is a wound.

Henceforth rich from the day of defeat,
I stand up to win your love.
We must go beyond our hatred
and search for ways to survive.

You've never seen the painful coming of the day
when the body is in torment.
You speak to it of love.
Of what love?
Of perhaps the one we leave on the wall
numbed with desire.

2 December

Baghdad
is a wingless bird
perched on the dream
that follows me like a sudden shower
and returns from whence it came.

Today Baghdad is everywhere.
And in spite of the cold
it is tracking me.

Wherever I go,
it is on me,
in me.
At times it keeps me warm
and sleeps with me.
It is the source of my pain,
it is my pain.

3 December

There are so many nights
we do not know
so much pain to efface
from one morning to the other.

Love uncontained,
so many small moons needed
to sweep away my desert,

so many tears to bear the dead,
to bear history and my cry.

So many small things to fulfill a dream,
and so much excess to keep our sanity.

So much insomnia to become a man,
and so much folly to be a martyr.

4 January 2000

Beyond your desire
I welcome you
and I embrace it

From the height of solitude
I shape your freedom,
and I become one with you.

Beyond my pain
I exist
and you,
you no longer know
if the day favours us,

or how to fashion the times of men,
or how to capture this cluster of days.

Yet . . .

[From 5 January 1999 to 4 January 2000]

FROM
The Open Sky of Baghdad

No. 1

After all those years of estrangement, I thought . . . like that ship imbedded in the rocks, like that flag set up on the hill . . . I thought . . . yes, perhaps . . . that there was a house in the city over there.

After the war, somewhere in a narrow street or in the mirror, someone would acknowledge me . . . A sister, a dead person, the remains of a father, a toothless brother . . . People would call me by my first name . . . or else someone I don't know missing an ear and without a smile would be waiting for me and would say:

'Your parents' home isn't here. You have to keep going.'

No. 16

I never thought I'd ride the wind
reach the hills
to survey the years
and understand how men
over there
cherished their wounds.

I think of the condemned
those who inhabit the cemeteries
and of others who
lacking a tomb
cling to a poem.

No. 17

Letter to my daughter, Inès

Yesterday, as night was falling
I gathered the remains of a broken moon,
sheets, frontiers, my fifty-one-year-old body,
a table without a sky, some poems,
letters without tears, names of assassinated comrades and
for you, my most tender thoughts.

10 May 2003

No. 18

I remember an immense night
where I hid my days, the desert, the hail
and a child's secrets
looking for submerged moments:
a broken toy, my wooden butterfly
the old window opening onto a wall
the barking of a stray dog at the moon
and a dawn held on leash

All is far off today
and the tyrant has gone

A seated wall remains
and its lassitude
keeping me company in a new obscurity.

No. 25

Everything is still to be done

Show me a horizon,
a window suspended over the sea

Stranger
I write to you from my exile,
I write to you with neither jasmine nor colour,
with your very words
born from our stones
from our arid land
a sky that resembles nothing

I address them to your merciless indifference
to your feelings of pride
paper kites in a sky
while my window yawns open over the void.

No. 29

To those who have already returned:
Don't forget the dead in exile
the forgotten valises filled with paving stones
with journeys unfinished
the humiliation of our own
lost in the everyday
in streets and in our maledictions.

Don't forget to iron out your lies,
to polish up your courage
to disguise the ruins of your life.

Remember, comrades
I too have seen
the sea and the sandy desert bird . . .

And when so many exiled are loaded with baggage
            and with tears
I wait . . . I wonder . . . I remain

I want to see from afar
what is happening in a city that no longer waits for me

To see what has taken my place
in my mother's eyes.

No. 30

Don't forget to lock away your loves
to shutter them
behind your days.

Don't forget to fold the garden
to pull out the seasons
to plough the sky
to shoot at the moon
to upset the stars.

Then once back in the country
take everything
and forget me.

No. 39

Where are the other executed
the other dead
their objects buried with the gentle wind of dawn
with love letters
and the lamentation of far-off memories?

My morning within arm's reach
there I put my days laden with exile
And in this mirror through torrents of rain
I ransack my body
and old age emerges
enwrapped in the silence of a sheet

No. 43

I am drunk with life
with this brutal day
thrusting itself onto the horizon of my thoughts

In the forest
I'll trace a path of dry branches
cry humanity
before . . .
savage and sudden
sinking into forgetfulness.

No. 50

How can I exhume my school bag
lost in the ruins of war
      on the way to seasons of happiness

Here, mornings open onto naked days,
without miracles
while over there each mirror is a face

Here one must rise up very early
over there death lies in wait for men

Here, mornings are covered with the fluttering of birds
over there, with the shattering of bodies.
Where is the man who knows how to smile
where is the keeper of the fruits of the earth?

Thirty Days after Thirty Years

Should I not name things
like a hand extended to one who's drowning,
like the unfolding of the seasons?
Have I not said
a thing always finishes at the expense of how its begun?

A flush of dust wends its way with an odour of childhood
while its procession carries off my uncertainty
slowly
gliding on the mainspring of the day.

I want to come close to you
bring you, in words, what the exiled has left undone

The dawn rises on Baghdad
and it consumes me.

My mother, like the light
needs no obscurity
just a little silence
when her son, the exiled, returns
settles on her branch
in the company of a star tattooed by the fog

For he's coming home
like a refugee passing through,
a fugitive looking to share
a smile

a piece of bread
a corner of a bed
and the witnessing of the drowned twilight

FROM

The Sweeper of the Desert

Inverted Mirror

My night is made of sand on a table of glass
I carry the odour of exile
my dwelling of clay is indeed there
without a garden, without a forest or a palm
my sky is an inverted river
and my words navigate
over a distant country
where men look for the day's direction

Those many nights I would run
until I muzzled emotions and wrung out the clouds
That soothed my spirit

Is my life still abandoned to waves that will not return?
And your own life,
and its dreams?

The Lost Dream

Often I doze on the shoulder of a wayfaring country
a land without virtue
I cannot boast
of the history of my ancestors

My ultimate desire
is to return from exile

No more rain in the gutter
no more clouds in the field
no more fish in the river
no more serenity at sunset
Since my nation is losing its love of man
what then will we talk about tomorrow with my old
mother?

Beautiful as Ever

It is your eyes
that made me grow up
in the cities of exile
where moons are born in secret
far from the eyes of assassins

I let my writing flow with the four winds

In revolt today
to defend life
without madness
I write on the door of tombs
where ashes keep the secrets

Darkness becomes the temple of my well-being
between 'to be' and 'not to be'
my call for help
is drowned in the infinite

After the Return to Baghdad

I had to renounce my dream to draw closer to you, that
dream I would maintain with strangers until I became my
own victim when the moments grew dense with memories.
I've arranged my feelings as one does in a familiar place
that's been abandoned. I've gotten even with the years of

regret. I've reproached destiny. I've opened the sluice gates of the river to hear what it was saying. Yes, I wanted to come back to you, laden with my existence like a believer who implores in vain. A believer who advances with the alphabet of the voyage on his tongue, the accents of his body, and who stands tall whenever he approaches a tomb.

But on the way
what to make of myself
and of the days' pain?

I've allowed nothing but nostalgia and hope escape from my thoughts. Finally, I'll become one with those places. Imagined places, lost places, like the shade of that tree at noon where long ago I'd drift off to sleep to grow up.

Mourning

Like a mother whose son has gone to war and who, at the outbreak of each morning, looks for the child's laughter left at the foot of a wall, we trace with regret those seasons that have neglected our sadness and caress joys so small that they have vanished.

Open the Window

Good morning mother
Early daylight suspended at the window

Good morning mother
I see you, unsteady upon awakening
I see your hope from now on under surveillance
To provoke the night soldiers
they need only to hear the clink of your rosary beads in the dark hallway
Do you think of me when men run away

leaving everything behind?
The nights jostle each other
with you a prisoner of their orbit
and me, captive of my exile
while you, dressed with that robe incrusted
    with tombstone flowers
in the light tainted by dust
you persist in filling the sacks of life
measure by measure

What does your morning look like now?
Did you sleep your fill like the other grandmothers?
Did you dream?
What verse did you choose to read before going to sleep?

I see your smile again
the clouds fastened to the wall
in memory of my defeat
and your eyelashes, wet, laden with dust
at the moment of our last farewell
That dream weighs on me, mother

Poem for Peace

I'm going to open the window
look down on the prairie of words
Let the dead stand up at the issue of the battle
let the prisoners return to their loved ones
and the war will be over

Then I'll close the window
take a place at the table
and put into order
what remains to be said
The exiled returns

like the seasons devoid of feeling
that no love awaits

The paths bark behind the hedges
the night's face is blurred
and a hand knocks at the door
of an abandoned homeland

Here the air makes the shadows tremble
with the flame of a candle
echo of horses galloping
cries of soldiers
and near oneself
a cold pillow

From the balcony of days
giving onto closed doors
I've long gazed at daybreak
on a flock unraveling in a mirage
while the moon wilted
in the heart of a young girl
raped

Then the evening returned
and with it
the child's fear
the thought
of meeting up with soldiers

Is it possible
that in a city
even destroyed by war
flowers will rise up from ashes?
The horizon flows over my heart
and at nightfall
plagues mark their path

The war has lasted many years
and all one hears is bitter moaning
as the sun sets behind the tanks

The Best of Words

Brothers, where should I begin my song?
I, the musician made of rain, the anonymous Baghdadien
the little night-school pupil
should I sing the mirage to the horses?
What to say then about the years of exile?

Perhaps I should begin with the Eden of your eyes
with your body leaning into the mirror
with the whistle of the train, of its smoke surrendered to
memory
or perhaps with the dust covering the shawls
    of the mothers in mourning
whose souls fasten the veil of their calamities

And if I were to start with the sky
with this moon of the poor
the round face of my mother
with her tender heart of the South
flooded with ashes by the rabble?

Ennui, Instant of Inspiration

For Hemadi

Listening to the victorious songs of cowards
like you I'm afraid that my ennui will crumble
Then the day gets drunk and my love closes its eyes
    on the horizon

If when you awake nothing in the morning satisfies you
look into the eyes of your beloved
and if you're alone
think about your country

Don't let your steps collapse
Don't flee
Let ennui surprise your existence
Sit down with it
And in spite of the light of the moon stained by wars
drink in its company to the chagrin of the absent
to infinite waiting, to frivolity

Share with it the memory of the drying up of the marshes
the thirst of children
and the dying of fish among the boats

It's not wrong to break down assassins' doors
        in the middle of the night
and to allow the dawn to diminish in a horse's eyes

Let the train turn over
for the sky has been blind since childhood
and the bar-room poets no longer amuse the ladies of
pleasure

Thus I observed you from afar
while a silver cloud
was honouring the solitude of the brave

Ephemeral Victories

We hastened our steps
towards the hoopla of the betrothal
while the day was announcing the funeral of the bride
        and groom

We came to the banks of the river
where the moon's shadow
caresses the solitude of motionless enclosures
and snuffs out the hesitant breath of our words

And when our feet touched exile
we rebelled against our homelands

They said: the tyrant has fallen
And while my head
barely escaped drowning
I hung our troubles behind the door
because here I was happy with the news

Then I found them again
playing dice, insulting each other
surrounded by a tumult of flies

Blindly, blindly
while on the sidewalk
others were filling sacks
with remains of bones
and anger was tearing at their soul

Blindly, blindly
I was trapped in my exile
like all those foreigners
devoured by nostalgia
Who will take me back to my dwelling?
Where are the canals and the water?
Where are the boats?

Then take a bit of a dream, my daughter,
before certainty leaves me
before sins assault me

Distressed dreamers
alone in their crossing
are like those lakes abandoned by pelicans
like those fish dying on the asphalt
that damage the clouds

They change course
and their destiny is launched
enough to sicken

Since yesterday
the sun is reflected in the river
flight has become the ritual of the villagers
Each one kills his moon in the wash
attaches a cord of fear to his neck
and hides the dawn
at the edge of a forest
of stubborn eclipses

War is Not a Lie

For my niece, Sarah, in Baghdad during the war

When the dune will be a mirage, Sarah,
and the horizon the light of wheat,
war will appear like a lie
escorting memory towards forgetfulness

What will bodies become?
What will I have left to offer you?
Words aged by anger
perhaps
but at least
far from the massacre

My former dream for man was a utopia

What word can you offer the soldiers
those who have disrupted your sleep?

From now on the stars lie dying in me
and I carry the homeland for you on my back
like a woven rug

Passionately

I no longer want to wait, with the seeping walls
for the winter of war

I, the child of unknown streets
moulded out of doubt and ennui
who searches for light
on the road taken by men

I traverse the morning on my knees
amid palms that are dying
I greet the horizon that meets infinite sadness
while anguish stagnates at the day's door and the sky
opens onto an invisible city

Lights meet in me
from the beginning
I ask: where is the frontier
and why does the bank where the lonely wind finds repose
overwhelm me with its cries?
Suddenly words of farewell are like a train
plunging into my body of clay

Let chance, things and nothings jostle each other
well-being will return
only after insomnia crucifies nights
painted with the foolishness of childhood

A few phrases
a little light
I look for an instant that suits me
rather than the obsessive language of exile
a language mixed with tears
then I say to myself:
The sky is out of sorts tonight
yet at dawn it will look down upon the cemetery
    of the hung

Fragments of files with the names of workers
who've been shot
white pages
tombs without roots
mutilated earth
multitude of bodies
sky opening onto absence
slowness of time
funereal wisdom, humid and cowardly
life without the demands of life

Excess
You speak, but what are you saying? A sunny night!
A farewell and handkerchiefs starred with tears
posed inevitably on the edge of autumn's parasol
recruit thoughts that hover over the soul's path
murmur the bitterness
of one departure after another, of one vigil after another
exhaustion, words without meter
and the pale language that accompanies death into its hole

The body will give up one of these winter mornings
after a visit to the dust
after the parade of the members that remain
and that of the heart

Will you then bring back to me the hour of the steppes
and the meditations on the sea?

Poem for Myself

If ever one of these mornings
your soul is crossed by a sad dawn
don't be afraid
You'll step away slowly

like the lament of childhood
The torment of the palm's shadow
still grows in the red clay of the Euphrates
It makes the flock of men
uncomfortable
their waiting even longer

Here men no longer remember the perfume of lavender
nor that of wax implanted in the flame

So root out the prison from your head
skin your body
perfume the look in your eyes
and with the fringe of light that remains
illuminate your exile
and repeat after me:
Passionately
strike down silence
cowardice

We need even more words and cutting acts
to defy the assassins
and save our dreams from their hatred

Baghdad is from nowhere
it is from here
it begins with me
and passes to others
and with them
it will remain

FROM
Seasons of Clay

Embarked

For Albert Camus

Write with the breath of one's homeland
with the clay of the liberated palm
with your steps rooted in the charnel houses of the poor

Write about the wind
that gives birth to drowned men

Write about the shoulders of the river
and also about the voyage from nowhere
at the moment that limits the day

Write like a prisoner of the mirror

Write to calm the universe in the head of a beggar
to extract the sap of memories

Write for migrating birds
and their unbroken flight

Write to illuminate a forest of devastated pines
and enlarge a tyrant's grave

Thus am I embarked on the body
of the tempest of men

Defeat

'What are you doing?'
'I'm looking at the morning of men.
'And exile?'
'What exile?'
One day, someone said to me: I suggest you get out of
your head. Well, for me, that was precisely what was
    terrifying.

The desert screams under my skin
'Deliverance!'
while winter grows like an immense window swallowing
the emptiness.
Snowflakes fall in me on a naked forest
like the bodies of dead butterflies on the forehead of
defeat

The deafening whistle of the wind escapes from
    my distress
like that of conquering soldiers

The absent mother's face remains
coveting the predatory time

'What are you doing?'
'I'm contemplating the night of men.'
'And exile?
'What exile?'

Shadow Figures

First shadow
It is three o'clock in the morning
I am pallid, definitively
and I seriously envisage leaving my skin

Second shadow
To rise very high in life
the ordinary man takes the escalator
while a cloud offers itself to the poet

Third shadow
We must leave to memory the right to choose its vocabulary
something irrational lies in wait for decrepitude
loss is inherent in the passing of time
the nostalgia of a passion escapes from it
and immediately returns

Fourth shadow
Early this morning I dreamt I was stretched out on a rectangular table. The light touched me, humid like a raw thought. I explained to my body the importance of the soul, its difference from the heart, from the mirror of the heart. Then I quickly turned to my left lung, to my liver and finally to my intestines. All agreed regarding the paralysis of my parts and, yet, I'm still not dead

Fifth shadow
I wonder up to what point the poem will keep its word
facing the lugubrious breath of the charnel house

Sixth shadow
You are my horizon
that radiance within the reach of my night

Yesterday? I Don't Remember!

It is so easy to trace an imaginary line
to cast the twilight with a sling
to have a friendly look
though attracted by a dead person
on a cold stretcher
In the cemetery
day becomes silent irrevocably
when the body is put in the earth
It is all so difficult to decode
the solitude of the trees in stones
and that moon suspended like an inverted lake
with its white light
on your breasts

On the other side of exile
you were there
and that dear penumbra
like a winter of childhood
at the very bottom of my page

Interrogation

Mother
what does the void cling to?
The hope of seeing you again
is a wound
which opens
onto an avalanche
of words

Moon of Clay

For Jean-Pierre Siméon

In the past was childhood
a little ragged
my urchin moon measured itself against the city
in a night without beginning
and with words indifferent to the desolate garden
and its shadow

I thought of the lost boat
planted in the red clay
One had to laugh at my vast wounds
whip the man who would not cry out
and walk
even without a dream
walk at the first age of light
towards a desert, there, in the street
left to the choice of a mutilated morning

Today I want a habitable world
without seductive rituals
without a sexed god

To live for something invented
a lie that's consoling
To riddle this wall in oneself
with words like embers

I salute you friend
up to the final pale deliverance of exile
up to my anguish
of a postponed life

No Regrets

Life is like that
it needs a cyclone
warmth
a little cold as well
for our hearts to continue beating

FROM
Baghdad-Jerusalem,
at the Fire's Edge

Unexpected Worries

Here I am close by the fence
vanquished
with my scars
and my old things

Here I am
I return to you
like a soldier who's never gone to war

Then don't ask me
the name of those who have fallen in battle
Don't ask how I've taken the path
to your dwelling

Know only
that I've not lost the sun
but that some scoundrels
stole it from me

Suffocation

1
My morning contemplates its existence
in the din of the city
What to do with the nostalgia
suspended on this age
like a jacket hung on the cord of regret?

And those assassins, over there
who divide up the body of the beloved!

2

In my exile
each evening
I return to this bed
immensity studded with extraordinary cities
with shell fish where the murmur of the sea
is still heard

And my old clothes
my jokes that remain at the bottom of a pack of cigarettes
the helmets of decapitated soldiers
the letters never read
the wars
I pile them at memory's door
I observe them through the night
while I look for you

Then with the steps of dawn approaching
as in the circle of years
I lose myself
without ever, in the end, reaching you

Always You

Where is the inheritance of exile
the fruit of the wind
and who will remember you
in the moments of joy?

You who move off
like a tormented storm
the happy cities will not weep for you

and on the way
look
the years weave forgetfulness
like bindweed
spreading over tombs

Nausea No Longer Has Meaning

1

I have not, like others, declaimed my poems
then why this nausea?

I've drawn woven stars
assembled them in my bed

In the heart of obscurity
I've said to myself, naively,
a belief in that cause
was enough to attain truth

I forgot their words were no more than sounds
of a senile tribe
of a herd of men
neutralized on the summit of dunes
and of horsemen who wipe their behinds
with sharp stones

2

When I emerged from the ribs of a people
incapable of living without defeat
I rolled up my sleeves
ate bitter fruit and dust
without ever prostrating myself before the tyrant

With the hunters, epic personae

I nailed stars to the void
invoked the celestial bull
and sterile dreams

Then I stood up in mourning
for the dead unknown to me
and I named the conquerors
assassins
and my tomb
the homeland

3

Do you not want to taste a little of my sadness?
You'll share with me the rising of the far-off moon
that grazes timidly
in the solitude of the herd

Do you not want to rest your soul
and at the two extremities of this earth
leave the gods to their own affaires?

You deny your imminent war
as well as your own person
and put your death bed
in the pocket of an old coat

4

You are worth more than this life
False paradises are forged
for poets who sow nonsense
who protect their skin from the slap of the cold

What's the good of showing off your dreams to me
me, a man bereft of bliss?

Yes, I missed that shower
also quit by the sky
But what will the star say to me
if I look at it with disdain?

A River on Paper

I plunge into the river
and emerge with the clay

On the shore I breathe in
enough air for a lifetime
then I sink into that clay
up to the root of being

Years
to search at last for a cure
for that river
for its bed

How many rivers, how many handfuls of clay
will I need today?

Not one promise has been kept
and even if the habit of writing poems
has not left me
each evening I fall into bed
like the darkness
for my wound
has not healed

At the Fire's Edge

For Ronny Someck

We stand
the day walled off

and the star of our childhood
sullied by the rabble
The moon
you know
is a deflated ball
for the poor children
from our quarters

Grass on the balcony has not grown
and I, ripe fruit,
age on the tree of exile
I have not been picked

As for you, your feet lead you where they will
and your head impels you where you don't want to go

You murmur in Hebrew about Baghdad
words emigrated from my heart
turtledoves taking wing
towards unknown islands

The palms bow in sadness for us
and finish buried by the secrets of eternity

Do not inhabit the darkness
approach the remaining light
be conscious in meditation
don't neglect the itinerary of the word

I cultivate my tomorrow
like a peasant
I strive to divert the storm
and listen to its improbable throbbing

In your eyes
a mirage

taking pleasure
in the hope that a country
will preserve its children from the abyss
Come
let us invent a poem
a guillotine for the killers
let us become a refuge
for lost time

Let us draw our mirage
on the walls
and put out tables
for our banquet

Here is your absent brother
burst forth from the book
He comes to you
his throat dry from shouting
In our countries
the living eat the dead
and the martyrs weigh no more than a few tears
So leave to their fate
the miserable adorers of God
accustomed as they are to bow deprived of their soul

Here I am like a bridge thrown over the abyss
little worried about righteousness
I gather up your shadow
I rescue you, forsaken star
and with the train of my exile
I lead you back to your original sky

Why does the wound
not bleed in our palms
in us, the crucified?

Even summer's perfume is frosty
and autumn no longer tolerates
the duplicity of poets
The trail of words
lies buried in the mud
It's not necessary
son of Mesopotamia
that we be the first
to erase frontiers

Let me rescue the east
for our ancestors
let me thwart the traps of hatred
and beautify the seasons of clay

My nostalgia travels now towards the Euphrates
It reaches your door
famished for love

My head's bound to the wall of exile
a window looking out onto dreams
a well without a shadow
only this grating
of the day's door

I no longer have a mother who waits for me
nor a turtledove
that weeps for me
the bats of my spirit
disperse
even now as the dust
falls again on my country

We'll reserve for later
the rest of the rain
we'll relate the story of the palms to our children

to their solitude
and we'll sing
for our dead
those who have prospered
in the depths of hell

For decades
I've raised up the night's canopy
turned the mirror around
its face to the wall
my throat, tepid
confronting death

Look, son of Baghdad,
I've known rough roads
covered over by sterile years
and now
rain dozes in the pores of the palms

Look how I draw a horse
facing the setting sun
neighing
in the middle of a dried up river
at an abandoned village
at its destiny
When your silence
in its serenity
takes flight
towards separation and its torment
I pronounce your name
and the borders are shut in my face
It matters little what the merchants of war
and the hypocrites
will say
clouds gossip in the streets of Baghdad
and assassins come from across the borders

Don't ever forget Iraq, your country
Come, join me
in striking down the walls
and cherishing the ashes
of our dead

There's no justice by the whip
and time shrinks us
with the growth of
life's absurdity.

Paper birds
sweep down
like the monsoon
Look
I throw a thorn
into the muzzle of nothingness

Together, let us tear out the tongues
that lie about peace
Let us incite them to revolt

[My affectionate thoughts also go to Samir Naqqash, Jewish writer
from Iraq, who died, exiled, in Israel.]

FROM
July Rain

Centred

On your knees
Yes
on your knees in the day's calm cruelty
and this endless absurdity
Walk, walk poor devil
into the extremity of the shadow
and rejoin your dreams
buried under their nights' laughable slowness

Leave your memories in tow
the dazzle of a deserted quay
and beyond
borrow the curve of your exile

The glory of the setting sun is there
without echo
alone on a stranger's bed
like a call from the highlands

Identity

I'm neither from Baghdad nor a poet
nor am I the shadow of a fig tree
but a divergence
the hint of a breath on the city
an uninterrupted conversation

Predator of chance
I observe nothingness, inexactitudes
I chase the enigma of the dream
my pain is composed of the ephemeral, the anecdotic
my days often dissolve in the quiet of the sunset
but I love you
and I learn quickly
as if in the dark

The Ambience of a Port

This morning
a cello inhabits the space
like a last letter addressed to the living

Must one repent?
become a bit of ash in the immensity of a tomb
an eroded cord for the tyrant?
Or should one see life like a dream
that's about to unravel?

The sea
that tear engraved in the window
memory slain
laid out in a shroud of light

Yes, I was born as late as a shadow in the desert
my idols are no longer
and of my god, honest but a troublemaker
I demand the uncertainty of narratives
and the whitening of bullets in the forehead of hate

Sadness Without Confession

Nostalgia awakes with the clarity of dawn
inspired
a sombre sky
a sad day
without confession
Manor
stumbling of age
a flash
inscribing the end in negative
at the heart of an uncertain desire

Origin of nothing
phantom of ink
conversing with a colorless field

Frost against the poverty
of an immobile future

Clay, white sand
infinity, approximated

Vertigo of petals
on a stomach, caressed
winter tide in the heart
without a tomorrow
kernel of an instant

for you, the words

All This

This bit of dusk
you bear in the wandering of the instant
this bit of horizontal light in time
it cuts, it penetrates you
like a face in the future
that dissolves into tears

Nothing but dampness now
your exile is drowning
and even the moon beams head for the beyond
This bit of inverted sky
like ink spread on a frosted field
scars of dreams that swell at the margins of your world

Vibrant wandering, I am within you
everywhere
you hold me like a sob in the heart of speaking
you ride me
you ride me to the end of the page

Appearance of Sense

In the reflection of the mirror
the morning's presence embraces the pearl of sense
the body's language
and even the obscurity of the room
accepts the irruption of another world

My sailboat sinks into the oily body of the night
precipitation into nocturnal language

Here, with words, resides beauty
here, dawn wipes its face
at the demarcation of nothing

To invent the essence of things
is a triumph over forgetfulness

FROM

*This Shower Comes from
Another Cloud*

Voluntary Transgression

To Albert Camus, once more

I write to you from my bewildered morning
I adjust the drowning to my sentiments
waiting for the tempest of my little dream of nothing
under the spell of this light
while you contemplate the whirling tornado

I want to tell you
that I spend my time playing with a rope
skipping over the dusty instants
and that I don't regret the memories
placed in me awkwardly
like stones

With forgetfulness in flower
like the look of a child who cannot speak
I hold myself like a wind
I cut up solitude
memory's inheritance of that autumn in writing
then the cruelty of the imposter swoops down upon us
like a last vengeance

Everything comes from afar
the voice and the embroidered dreams of returning
that star flirting with the window
and even the fear of being bombarded
like the mother who remained in the war
Yet the moon no longer recognizes the assassinated

and the alienation of the men from here
no longer amuses the exiled

I write to you
because I cannot grow accustomed to cowards
who have never known nostalgia

I write to you
about my pain
before a pirated France
in this mutilated library

and yet I want to die here
despite the imperfection of the dawn
despite the books and their authors
from now on
packed away

This Shower Comes from Another Cloud

1

In this vast night
unthinkable to retain the sea with one's hands
dry the wound of the seasons
put the desert in one's pocket
tattoo the dawn with cries
and invent another life
for these limping words

To see you again?
To vault over the shadows
like the moaning of weeping women
remembered by partisans

2

Must I bury myself in the mirror of solitude?
I am the witness of exile
of our ill-used dreams

What is on the outside
is inside me
I have no poems like the Medusa
that petrify
no poems to root out of my notebook

Exile is my homeland
not my dwelling

I'm the echo of the river
suspended over a feverish memory
To till your breath
I offer myself to the fiery shower
that swallows the blue mountain
in landslides of writing
and I revive the look of the last Bedouin.

Baghdad, Desperately

To depart without leaving one's self
simply to look at the blue of the sea
and absorb the flesh of the sky

Not to flee one's night
on an inert boat

To depart is not to look ahead
but to correct the wearing of time
to trim the seasons
To depart does not mean to chase the moonlight
but rather the dawn barking in man

For it's here
that the shower hides the shadow of Baghdad
like the return from a long voyage
like a dark season
cadenced by mourning

Distance comes in little waves
and fixes itself like a wing on my morning

Then I go out
I walk
I get up
in the blinding light

And I sway
like a winter lost in its own mist

Beginning of a Ceremony

For Robert Lobet

Happiness, inert, at the end of the wind
cafe to the south
attached like a lighthouse behind a blur of tears

No, friend
another world does not exist

Here, nothing but what is necessary
centuries passed joined to stones
Dawn is dead
as is the butterfly
terrified by the ugliness of the vanquished

The night, an old swing
bows down before the madness of the immensity
and trembles
like an island stranded among trees

I told you
the country has not washed my face for the past forty years
It sleeps in a hangar like the assassinated
across from the fallen palm in the mirror

I told you
I've preserved all those ruins
and even this rage

As in a Dark Dream

Like a dog in the distance
the night barks
Its voice traverses the marshes of childhood

I forgot my face
the echo of dried-up wells
the moon of my mother sacrificed to the war
as well as the burning of my tongue

Behind the deep crevices of the stone
I see the skeleton of my father
his mouth awkwardly sculpted in the clay
like a wound in the winter

Seasons of Incertitude

Issued from my river
highlands eroded by spots of fertile dryness
men cover themselves with dust

Since then
I dig tirelessly
with my voice in the silent flesh of the light
To catch a cloud
by chance
in the actual
Break definitively with the ultimate solitude

Along the seasons of incertitude
seated at the summit of humanity
I shake the surface of a sleeping lake
gaping scar

Lying on the flag of our fathers who died for nothing
I teach the child in me
to decipher waiting
I exist
but don't know the secret of torment
nor the realm of a father's solitude

From here I hail my wounded morning
like the indigent moon
a far-off country
I sift through the tricks of Tayhe the abandoned dog

I seal the imagination of crickets
and follow the horse that invades the sunset
I applaud the slowness of night birds
and the irreversible utopia
Then I dance like a weak star
behind the slaves' enclosure
I tend to the beak and the word
bestir the soul of the migrant
and the dawn of my return to Baghdad grinds
like the wings of a condor
praying in a gigantic tree

FROM

Season of Salt

Mother of the Morning

For Jeanne Rolland, from a son who has never stopped loving you

The hills cradled by the horizon
cluster in a shipwreck beyond measure

I see you
lofty soul
where the twilight abounds

Long ago
I was the palm grove
that trembled under your wings

In our seasons
your tender hands embroidered the years
and in your eyes
one saw the day appear

You were the hour glass of my mornings
and I named you life
river bank that tended my wounds
dawn that lent me a hand in the penumbra

With you the years were reversed
the horizon, upset
faced a hill of angry words
or those that jostled each other
without meaning
Thus once again I call to you
seagull hovering on high
do not forget our destiny

If Baghdad gave birth to me
France made me a man

The exile that has nourished me
is exhausted from the intensity of the dream

Happy the one who, like you, crosses over
joyful at approaching the nearby shores
where unfaithful memory
sometimes withdraws
and disappears
like the tide

Homage

Write
like the trembling bird
that reinvents the rhythm of flight

Write
aiming high
to say the sea
at the horizon
empty of migrating birds

Write for the Arab in revolt
and denounce the sky of the believers
sealed off like a tomb

Then cherish a long time
that silence inherited from my mother

Nebula

While you sleep sheltered from yourself
everything is deformed, rushes in
One's heart becomes anonymous in the fog

Everything flies off after the jolt of age
except my body
and my mother's star that watches over my illusions
lost in this city devoid of minarets

Troubling for an instant,
this face, reduced under the storm
this inclining body
its nerves on the look-out

One examines this day made of porcelain
a boat on the causeway
and without warning
Baghdad and I lose ourselves in Paris

Here, the smells, the immensity of carbonized dreams
Everything moves in me, the road, the houses
and the plastic roses of she who is absent
My bruised childhood is no longer dead
and the Euphrates as well
runs the length of my soul
very far from the suburbs
bathed in twilight

Kite

It's enough to display the autumn
to read in the morning
like a kite tossed in a sky
far from its native land
A fractured space
that writes of the lassitude of absence
Will it be a warning for the tyrants?

In place of words
at this moment
the sky has disappeared
for ever separated from the instant

Days confront each other
and defend themselves

Ruptures in the breeze of dust
Mutants in retreating nature

But who will be godfather to my existence
this almost useless phenomenon?

FROM
Mirage

Obstinacy of exile
where words plunge the voice into darkness
mass of nights
culminating in a mute dawn

And my Calvary extends
with this long line of the dead
boundless
until it holds foolishness on a leash

. . .

It's for me to interpret thirst
the reality of dried-up marshes
the faces of writing
and the moon tormented by the bow of the wind
dying behind the groves of palms

Obscure zone
reticence of words clandestinely engraved
in a conversation of foundered bodies
where silence becomes celestial

. . .

When I awake in an unclear morning
I say to myself:
How imprudent to be a poet confronting the torturer!
These times, my love, lend reason to masks

How imprudent as well
to trust chance
to hide behind inspiration
that justifies ordinary language
and to submit to the erosion of time!

    . . .

I wake up within you, free
without a destination, without an echo of returning
I become my own country
a cemetery for dreams
for the tombs of my father and mother
and I wear clothes of the Aïd
destined for orphans

    . . .

In the drowning of the twilight
and in the mist of the shadows
there's neither mirage
nor blue sand
nor a growing truth
The rebellious light hides
unpunished
It lodges in a mirror
without tomorrows
like a little wing given up to panic

FROM

Rebuild the Days
Poems from Marrakech

For Lucille Bernard and François Gache

Unfinished Word

Come visit me
with your broken wings
in the lacuna of insomnia

You rue your sins
In your bed
the paralysis of exile

Then, my beloved, explore
the secrets of the orphan
and of dreams receding into the dusk

Come visit me
when the butterfly
in its madness
goes between the damp fields of daybreak
and the tender flesh of the light

Despite this mirage
ugliness wearies my heart
and drowns my desert in silence

Meditations

People's ignorance is an exile
and freedom in exile
is one's country
We must understand the meaning of our acts
to do away with the cruelty of others

It's difficult to grow a tree in nothingness
for a spring always runs
between the hardness of the rock
and the root of life.

. . .

Celebrate the inheritance of pain
from the suspended dream
and as it fades
leave silence
undisturbed

. . .

Speak out
like breathing
and embrace life

Debris of Memory

Writing
is as vast as the look of a magician
an invisible point of time trampled on
adrift on a hillside of palms
an attempt to approach the horizon

A new place
a new rock
and the suspicion that exile is my dwelling
Baghdad
Do you hear the call from the valley
the interrogation that shatters words?

Low Sky

One day I'll be a poet
and my fake angels will fly over
impossible dreams

Here, like a spear facing an enemy
I whip my paper horses
Will they in the end track men down?

I was there, before the flood
I commanded the slaves
to make the ship move forward
I joined the gypsies on the dunes
well before the arrival of the rat-men
those that destroyed the twilight of the poor

Word after word
I strive to fulfil my destiny
to cherish the fragile instant of the forgotten light

But he who wants to think
must explain the inhospitality of the world
like the story of my father
buried under a rain of stones

Inundation

The sky this morning speaks wisdom
a lazy prayer in the intimacy of age
In the rush of the cycle of life
even regrets have abandoned sorrow
Long confession
on the tragedy of my departure
mysterious jungle

How to rebuild the days
since the sun of childhood
floats on the sadness of the snow
a gap in the memory of whiteness?

Breathless words
stuttering of the void's abyss
posed like an armful of roses on my bed

They talk of absence
and of the river

Itinerary

The land belonged to those who had departed
under the thunder
and the nakedness of the palms in the burning air
resembled the springtime of the man in flight

From dusk to dawn
only the depths of the desert
are equal to your solitude

Daily Bread

With the imagined words of the other
the remains piled high
of this postcard life
and with the poem missing
tell me how to reconstruct a country

Rebuild the Days

If they listen to my call on the threshold of the summer
I'll tell them how dreams finish off one's heart
how lost nights open onto
the dispersion of days

Rebuild those days
to confront an announced vanity
a stoned spring

Rebuild the days
on bended knee
fascinated by existence
by a cry from childhood
lost in the war

My expectation
captured by a confused spirit
withdraws
and traverses the rain on the hill

Rebuild the days
as if all were ready
Those times tattooed on clay
the incense, the violin, the voice and the flute of sorrow
and still
you did not come
your shawl embroidered with sand

We were the living dead
silent in the entrails of pain

Memory of a defeat
where people were running
I looked for you among the hung
and the faces of demonic soldiers

Rebuild the days
with the breeze
and our habits
the dawn reappeared
penetrating the void
and I gave way

Rebuild the days
on bended knee
with the ripening of prohibited fruit
I bare myself
despite this insane downpour
that soaks the soul of the dead

Rebuild the days
on bended knee
while the horizon drowns in the swelling of the sky
and nothing is left of the forest
but a carbonized clearing
I'll be of the generation that walks backwards
carrying its ark on its head

[Riad Sahara Nour, Marrakech, May 2012]

FROM
Adieu, My Torturer

• From **'THE CRICKETS' GAME'**

. . .
For a long time, I've retraced paths
I name the seasons as I wish
I destroy cities, I bury men
I weep over the past
I construct villages with sheet-metal roofs and treeless
prairies
I wash tombs of ghosts without wings
I dismantle shrouds in search of a country and a faithful
friend

I'll not pronounce my last word
I need neither a god nor a frontier
And like men deprived of bread
I demand freedom

. . .

I would so like to close the voice of the mirror, no longer look at either the age of the body or the age of reason. It's always so late in my winter. In my writings. it's no longer cold but it's raining in me.

. . .

I am the nomad accompanying his own story. I walk under a sky crackled like dry mud embedded with mirages. I am the improbable mystery followed by the improbable caravan itself loaded with words and truths.

. . .

Before the frontier of civilizations, my words shout out and make peace resonate. If no one feels concerned, at least I will, while other men are caught up in the race to death. Kill anything, anyone. Kill, simply kill. Why in the world do I think of Halabja, that village eviscerated by Saddam Hussein, the Arab tyrant? Why didn't my Arab brothers condemn the massacre of those Kurdish peasants? Arab thought was dishonoured. Authorities of high rank and dignitaries of the Arab world overflow with assassins and renegades. It makes me sick.

A Kurdish writer came over to ask a question: 'You, an Arab poet, what do you think of Halabja?'

We wept together during those cheerless times. He as a Kurd and I as an Arab, we were both victims of Saddam's dictatorship and we escaped from the same cemetery to be resuscitated on a Paris pavement.

. . .

Long ago, when I was in the military, the truck from the barracks had driven us, the other soldiers and me, up to the entrance to the woods . . . Then the young man of twenty that I was found himself leaving the woods, a rope around his neck, surrounded by soldiers, bare-chested, covered with mud. The military camp with its prisoners stretched out as far as you could see and I said to myself that between the obscurity of the torturers and the precarious light of God, all that was left to me, as a victim, was to run towards the void.

. . .

Why doesn't your soul find peace like a cloud that moves
off without regret
I, the victim, I waited for you and you didn't come
They've torn away my clothes
Violated my nights
Closeted the misfortune of my exile
They've set fire to my history
And you didn't come

. . .

Oh my country, do you sense our humiliation?
For how long will you let yourself be guided by ignorance?
Are you the blind one who searches warily for the meaning
of his life
Among the errors and obscurity of his history?
I will not perish in the streets of unknown cities
As the assassins would like it
I'll hang onto the edge of words
I'll say farewell to you

. . .

After the destruction of bridges
And the bodies that pile up
then disperse like foam
I've had enough of your solitude
Of the assassins' celebrations
Of the shouting by militants
Who prepare their tombs in oblivion

. . .

After covering myself with shame

I have not changed
My dwelling is my tomb
And my body, my country.

. . .

The sky is low, a wall toppling into the void, a wall of glass traversed by gentleness while the light from the horizon, like a torrent, tumbles down. Mother, where are you? Where is our house? I can no longer see the bus stop where you used to wait for me amid a tumult of people. Light from those old days is as fragile as a bubble.

. . .

When will my thoughts be free of this endless exile? Will I one day be cured of this sickness of loss provoked by my torturer?

. . .

How I long to see those who are far from me . . . It's with ink and words that speak of my suffering that I recompose a family for myself.

How to free myself from this nostalgia?

I'll sculpt dates, wheat, salt. I'll graft a heart onto them, one that beats like mine, overflowing with this same nostalgia, with kindness and with hope and sacrifice. I'll call them my family. I'll beg their aid when I'm afflicted or have lost faith in the road of existence. I'll bite into them like a banished dog that finds a bone right in the middle of life's emptiness. Then I'll greedily devour them . . .

No one served as an example for me. Not even my father. I made this life with my own hands, without sacred books, without a mosque, without devotion to a prophet or a god . . .

. . . it's with my head high that I approach the horizon of existence. I abandon without regret tears, sombre memories of offences and misery. The beliefs of those men will sink into the sands of my room. Then all that is old will be dispersed by waves and carried off to unknown shores like two lovers that separate . . . one falling from a vertiginous height and the other suspended, the solitary witness of the fall of his double into the abyss of an obscure memory.

. . .

Here are the years that have passed tattooed on a skin that will never be mine. My age is definitively burnt by exile despite the fall of the torturer. An age consumed in cities covered by the dust of shooting stars with dirty sleeves. I do not want to be a Rimbaud, trafficking in slaves, or a Neruda who has left only a song on the lips of those who suffer. I want to be a gentle quietude that streams like sweat on the forehead of forgotten men. May it fill with hope those arms that cling to distant horizons.

. . .

What can a child say to his mother after thirty years of exile and forced absence, after fifteen years of silence imposed by the dictator? I had left as an adolescent; I was returning old. What can we know of sentiments? How do we question the lost words and years? How do we approach the unknown? What do the victims have to say? Where to start? What does absence mean?

How can we free the mother from the exiled one?

. . .

This family the dictator has dispersed is together now after many years. Somewhere in this insane world, we are seventeen sailors hounded by the cold and the storm, who huddle around a poor fireplace. Lost, thrust about by our thoughts, we fix our gaze again at the new spark born from the embers. And as if we were leaning over a high balcony, we perceive far in the distance the waves in the sea that bury all, as they advance towards us.

How can we make men free?

. . .

Oh, my Baghdad, my torment. How small is your sepul-
ture and how immense, your pain! You knock on the door
of my writing to help me get well, to mend the lack of loving
words for you. How could I forget you? How could I forget,
while reason dictates that my mortuary shroud will be my
body's last prison . . .

. . .

One day I was a young man. Before that, I was a child.
What do I have to remember? . . .

. . .

They say the tomb is only a place. We'll enter it after
finishing with our dreams, those of our exile. According to
them, to live this exile is as simple as leaving one's home to
relieve oneself in an abandoned field and return! Thus I'll
have simply walked around in the light of day to come back
once the night has fallen. Must this be the way to describe
the sentiments of the one who has dragged his existence in
the rotten waters of separation? Of the one who has seen
his years consumed far from the faces of loved ones?

. . .

Because I also have the impression of having left people
to their tombs while I vaunted my importance. Yet I knew
that my painful effort wouldn't be enough to make the

universe go round and that the illusions of my youth were as frail as one of my miserable days.

. . .

Dreams started to decay in my soul. Those dreams that never left me as I was growing up proved to be, after all, inaccessible.

. . .

Exile has grown accustomed to me and I've grown accustomed to it . . .

I'll drag my dwelling, I'll haul it up to the sea
Over there
I'll put it on a little dune
And each morning
I'll sit on its doorstep. I'll observe what life has done
    to me
That detail on my face for example was all I'd
    inherited from
my father
It didn't help me pass the frontier
I put it in a sack with that father
And we started our crossing

For all these years I've wept over its destiny
I never ceased repeating to myself:
The war will be finished and the people will get even
    with the torturers
You will marry and have children
Then you'll return to your country
Relate your story
But no one will believe you
For no one is waiting for you

. . .

My father, may his soul rest in peace, wasn't convinced of the utility of life. Like most men in our country, his spirit had been violated by the tyranny of the State and religion . . .

. . .

. . . Today, I fully understand that life was not kind to him. That's why, despite the burden of his irresponsible ways, I think of him and my love is rekindled for ever.

. . .

No one will erase the noble reasons for my exile. Yet little huts emerge beyond a village in a valley enveloped in clouds. Yes, I've harbored an immense nostalgia for the country that imprisoned and tortured me and that, today, no longer recognizes me.

. . .

You, the tyrant, have been entombed for just a few days while I, because of you, have been wasting away there for years. I don't want to converse with your soul while the memory of your cruel look is still so keen and the echo of your wicked laugh is still too present in me . . .

. . .

I spent the entire day walking. For many hours, I forced myself to put up with my melancholy and the darkness of my soul. Even the clouds held back their élan and the day resembled an orphan dressed in his Sunday best. I moved along dragging my solitude. An intense emotion made me suddenly shiver. I was thinking of those villages shimmering in a distant mirage. No one was waiting for me there now . . . Then, from my tomb, tyrant, I saw you approach yours . . .

Your end awakened me from a profound and sick sleep. I finally understand, without the least effort, that I no longer have a need of poems. Yet, I'll need to write something else for, without writing, I risk becoming like you, a man without compassion, even for myself.

. . . Solitude envelops me at the foot of the dictator's tomb. His body has been wrapped in a cloth printed with three insignificant stars and stained with the blood of millions of victims. I no longer see anything in this place but fallen men lamenting.

Oh Baghdad, I no longer expect anything of you! I no longer look into the distance, no longer dream of a return of that far-off time. But I'll always remember the feet of that child playing in the waves churned by the boats sailing on the Tigris. I'm going to close my writing on that city and its inhabitants. I'll offer a new horizon to my exile made of dunes, of frontiers and of elegies. I'll create a refuge that fits me, make my companions the planets issued from my imagination. I'll reinvent that poor moon which floated above the huts of the villagers . . .

. . .

. . . Here I am stripped of everything except my spirit of revolt. I walk next to the hoard of assassins . . . At times I run to rid myself of the coldness of their sentiments, indifferent to the rain thickening the air. And despite catastrophes, I keep advancing, leaving them wondering over my absence. Yes, alone, I'll imagine the end I deserve. And before dust fills my throat, I'll do what I must so that my death is worthy and in no way resembles that of the tyrant whom abject men present as a hero.

FROM

For You, I Dream

For Lou, my granddaughter

A poem which sculpts in words
the story of a man who came from afar
to begin a new life in France, a land he cherishes.

Our hands remaining on the fire
have not brought Summer back
to the turtledove frozen in pain.

For you, I dream
the moon clings clumsily
to the summit of the palms
memory of the beyond
like a night encircled by forgetfulness . . .

For you, I dream of time in the slow motion of reverie
caught up in a whirlwind of white sand.
. . .

For you, I dream the moon of my mother,
born from the seed of nothingness
her life made of chance
a life of lamentation
from Paris to Baghdad
before doors
torn off

For you, I dream
a sharing of the bitter snow
your sunrise watches over a lost thought

For you, I dream of my besieged soul
of that little Aïd lost before the exile
of that step that crossed an offended continent
. . .

For you, I dream of the darkness which clings to my fingers
patch of blood against patch of night
dream against the rack's torment
. . .

For you, I dream of that downpour
spreading into the shadows
of the questioning that bolsters the failing memory
. . .

For you, I dream, my love
of the embers that forge words
I dream too of a furrow in the human heart
May those who have been abandoned
at long last, smile!
. . .

For you, I dream of an endless light
of age that no longer advances
but that runs
of the slowness of the torturer to execute the partisan
of those traces of accumulated silences
in the numbing void
. . .

For you, I dream of a senile desert
of moaning wind
of a forest without arms
of everywhere, all around
keen-edged blackness
encircled by dunes
and by a sun
descending tirelessly
on men
. . .

For you, I dream of a light in the hollow of the wall
of the immobility of cowardly men
of a lukewarm night
from nowhere
. . .

For you, I dream of that desolate swing
between two palms
of my first poem, torn up
in my prison cell
of the camp's heavy smoke
of the men behind the barbed wire
and their mute eyes
looking up to the horizon

For you, I dream of my lamentation
breathless in the labyrinth of words
I dream of the odour of my time
of my reconciliation with death
. . .

For you, I dream of my dream that suffocates
on the disfigured road where they burn poets
I dream of the sleeping valley
of the stars moaning in the cold

For you, I dream of the moon that comes up
over the ruins of writing
like a prostitute bartering my exile
with smugglers of death

For you, I dream in the valley of age
transfigured by chance
One abandons frontiers

hunts down forgetfulness
no longer recognizes
words or men
. . .

You'll enfold dreams, pale and slow
in our shadows,
a mystery
frost on the lips of dreams
a mouth broken in the echo of your laughter
Thus my words and your voice will remain
beating the borders of desire

For you, I dream the horizon
a gentle handkerchief
embroidered with joy

But the poem, the citadel of breath
from where does it come?
. . .

From cascade to cascade
nights upon nights
snow in Summer
stolen Springs
death confronting death
up to the giddiness
of a new birth

Notes

PAGE 1 | *Above the Table, a Sky*

Translated into French by Salah Al Hamdani in collaboration with Elizabeth Brunet Sancho.

PAGE 7 | *Memory of Embers*

Translated into French by the poet and Elizabeth Brunet Sancho.

PAGE 9 | BUNDLE OF DAYS OVERWHELMED BY THE WAR

A series of twenty-nine poems, one for each day.

PAGE 9 | 'The Fourth Day'

Fakhati: A bird in Iraq, well known for its appearance in popular myths associated with the theme of sadness and nostalgia.

'The Sixteenth Day'

Desdasha: Djellaba in the Arabic of Iraq.

PAGE 13 | I'VE SEEN

These are fragments that appeared in *Memory of Embers*, translated into French by the poet in collaboration with Elizabeth Brunet Sancho (1993). The poet produced a complete edition in French (2001), in collaboration with Isabelle Lagny. These translations are based on the 1993 text except where noted.

PAGE 13 | 'gatherings bound to memory': From the 2001 edition.

PAGE 13 | 'and skylarks burdened with bundles': From the 2001 edition.

PAGE 13 | 'Norouz': Spring and New Year for the Kurds [note from the 1993 edition—Trans.].

PAGE 14 | 'an abandoned lighthouse': From the 2001 edition.

PAGE 14 | 'scattered in a cemetery of days': From the 2001 edition.

PAGE 15 |'in the language of Baathists': The Iraqi National Socialist Party, headed by Saddam Hussein that caused the destruction of the Iraqi nation and its people from 1968 until today [note from the 1993 edition—Trans.].

PAGE 15 |'I'm like a heart that burns,': From the 2001 edition.

PAGE 15 |'The chateau of no return': A penitentiary in Iraq where they torture, assassinate, with the reputation of never allowing those who have entered it to leave [note from the 1993 edition—Trans.].

PAGE 16 |'curses fly up from an illuminated page': From the 2001 edition.—Trans.

PAGE 16 |'of the uprising of March': Refers to the uprising against the fascist regime in Iraq in March of 1991 where hundreds died [note from the 2001 edition—Trans.].

PAGE 16 | EPILOGUE

From the 2001 edition.—Trans.

PAGE 21 | *The Arrogance of the Days*

Published in Arabic in 1996 as *The Height of the Days*. Translated into French by Said Abdul Sahib. Revised by Isabelle Lagny and the poet in 1997.

The English translations of 'Baghdad, Twelfth Look' (as 'XIIth View'), 'The Beacon of Makeshift Houses', 'The City of Sand', 'A Homeland' and 'The Necrologist' were first published in *Metamorphoses* (Autumn 2011).

PAGE 23 | MEN

PAGE 24 |'The Eleventh Man'

Dedication, For al Saggar: Mohammed Saïd al Saggar (b. 1934), Iraqi poet, calligrapher, playwright and inventor of the Saggar alphabet. Living in exile in Paris since 1978.

Bassora: Rebellious and martyred city in the south of Iraq.

PAGE 27 | THE HEIGHT OF THE DAYS

PAGE 28 | 'The Tenth Day'

Dedication, Jawad Bashar: Iraqi cinematographer exiled in France.

PAGE 34 | MY BLACK FLOWER

'The Necrologist'

Dedication, For Ghanem Hamdoun: An Iraqi journalist.

PAGE 83 | *The Open Sky of Baghdad*

PAGE 90 | 'Thirty Days after Thirty Years': First published in English by the translator in *Baghdad Mon Amour* (Curbstone Press, 2008).

PAGE 93 | *Sweeper of the Desert*

PAGE 95 | THE ILLUSION OF PRESENCE

Translated into French from the Arabic (Iraq) by the poet and Isabelle Lagny.

PAGE 104 | AN EXILE AS BIG AS A MIRAGE

Poems written in French.

PAGE 133 | *July Rain*

These texts, published between 2010 and 2012, were reprinted in *Rebuild the Days*, 2013.

PAGE 153 | *Season of Salt*

PAGE 155 | 'Mother of the Morning'

Dedication, Jeanne Roland: Al Hamdani's mother-in-law who helped him learn to read and write French. She was a mother figure for him in his early years of exile.

PAGE 161 | *Mirage*

PAGE 164 | Aïd: Festival that ends Ramadan.

PAGE 177 | *Adieu, My Torturer*

Translated into French from the Arabic (Iraq) by the poet with Isabelle Lagny.

PAGE 191 | THE MAN WITH THE WICKED LAUGH

Translated into French with the collaboration of Saïd Sayagh.

PAGE 193 | *For You, I Dream*

Dedication, For Lou, my granddaughter: Salah Al Hamdani's first granddaughter.